THE SUCCESS EXPERIMENT

THE SUCCESS EXPERIMENT

FLEXMAMI's formula for knowing
what you really want and how to get it

LILLIAN AHENKAN

LOST
THE
PLOT

Contents

This one's for the doers.

Introd

uction

WHAT THIS INTRO *WILL* TEACH YOU

How this self-development book can help you achieve your goals

How to define, understand and improve your self-awareness

How to think critically

What manifesting is (and whether you need to be spiritual to do it 'properly')

WHAT THIS INTRO *WON'T* TEACH YOU

How to prioritise instant gratification over long-term success

How to make unrealistic vows to increase productivity and decrease procrastination, only to burn out and lose motivation

How to become a different person for the sake of self-betterment (the goal is simply to be a better version of you)

I don't think there's an easy or magical path to self-betterment. But I do believe there are certain tools, processes and mindsets that can help make the journey a hell of a lot smoother.

This book will show you how to assess and overcome the factors that have been getting in your way and preventing you from getting what you want. And of course, teach you how to achieve your goals. That's why you're here, right?

I define self-betterment as the process of improving yourself mentally, physically, spiritually or emotionally, in ways that push you closer to a personal goal. Whether that be learning a new skill (carpentry! No? Just me?), diving head-first into a dream career (and hoping you don't drown under the pressure) or packing up everything and travelling the world (first class is preferred, but my budget won't allow for anything more than economy).

What drives people to be better? Why do we bother? What does improving yourself really look like? Your reasons are probably ever evolving — big one day and small the next. Maybe you're looking to fill a void, inject some excitement into your existence, or just do something different. Maybe you have a dream that feels unattainable. Maybe you're looking to take control and start living the life you dream about. These desires change as you change, and transform as you transform, and similarly, the steps you need to take to get to where you want to go won't always be intuitive, clear or straightforward. Unfortunately, there's no one-size-fits-all approach to getting closer to your goals. **True self-betterment requires a mindset shift, which then helps you to create unique guidelines, made for you, by you.** A good place to start is by ridding yourself of some unhelpful thinking patterns.

As you already know, there are heaps of external barriers to success, including but not limited to your status, society, glass ceilings, your upbringing, the patriarchy, intergenerational trauma, nepotism and all the other structures and experiences that have negatively impacted you on an individual level. How you feel about those barriers, and the way they've disrupted your journey, is valid and important, but unfortunately, **they exist and are out of your control**. Take a moment to sit with that thought. It might instinctively make you feel deflated or demotivated — but it shouldn't. Learning about how these structures affect you and your approach to life should definitely be a high priority. Start using Google to research, talk to your peers, look within — but once that's done, what's next? Do you throw in the towel? Resign yourself to the idea that you'll never truly get what you want? Or do you buckle down and give it a red-hot go anyway?

This is your chance to start focusing on the things you can improve, instead of looking towards the negative.

The Success Experiment has a simple-enough premise: through learning, understanding and nip-tucking a few internal factors, like your personality, attitude, beliefs, perspective, habits and resilience, you can cultivate skills which will help you achieve all your goals, to get whatever you want. Although, there are no promises that will be the same now as at the end of the book. These changes won't erase the barriers put in your way, but you may find that they lessen the impact of some of the structures causing havoc in your life. And don't try to tell me you've exhausted all your options, because I've gathered a book's worth of ideas for you to try on for size.

You may be wondering what qualifies me, Lillian Ahenkan (aka FlexMami), to write this experiment. Somewhere between aggressively studying the habits of successful people and trying to will fame and excessive amounts of disposable income into my life, I discovered a gap in the self-help market. I'm a huge consumer of self-betterment wisdom myself but, in recent years, many of the books I've turned to lacked relatability and accessibility for someone my age, and for someone who simply wants the things I do: a sometimes-superficial, realistic and self-sustaining approach to success. I needed a few less references to business models and a bit more pop culture. **I needed to be reminded that my wants were valid, even if they weren't traditional.** It's not that I necessarily want my personal development information to come from a millennial. But I found myself looking for someone to assure me that, even though they didn't know me personally, they had an idea of what I — and other people in my generation — want and need. That they understood the unique challenges we may be facing. Who's writing for the average person with above-average goals? For people with progressive (and perhaps unconventional) ambitions? Who understands that for some, a decade at university would probably reap benefits, but that others probably prefer to do their learning on Google? The perfect self-betterment book for me would have all the sciency data for legitimacy, but also include just a bit more *fun*. So I decided to write that book — the book I needed — that took the best of the conventional but made it my own. Hopefully, it will turn out to be the book some of you need too.

If you've read some of what's out in the market and haven't yet found advice that resonates with you; if you're looking for a new way to get inspired; if you have your own goals but no idea how to achieve them or where to look for guidance: this book is for you.

I'm popularly known as Flex to most, FlexMami to some, Lil to very few and Lillian Ahenkan to even fewer. I'm a two-time uni (private college and TAFE, to be specific) dropout with poor time-management skills and a serious sense of career FOMO, which means I'm always doing too much. Burnout is a close mate of mine. I find it difficult to create habits that are good for me. I can be shocking at follow-through if things aren't lining up as I imagine — I'm a big-picture person. Mostly, I just want to get from A to B as quickly and easily as possible. I'm a jack of some trades, a master of even fewer, and have been known to cut corners for the sake of productivity. Despite being a highly imaginative and creative person, I can be a realist to a fault. Yes, I love fantasising about alternate realities and all the possibilities, but I also hate getting swept up in my own delusions if they're not likely to happen. If morality is binary, then I believe people are more inherently bad than good, which is not a 'bad' thing, but it definitely influences how I see the world (a lot more than people realise). I can be really sceptical, distrustful and I often want to know why people are the way they are and how this influences what they say, think and experience. I think everyone has an agenda, and the sooner I can figure out how you think, the sooner I can figure out who you are.

I've become pretty good at setting boundaries and building relationships based on transparency. I'm still working on managing my expectations of myself and others; sometimes I set the bar unnecessarily high, and other times it's ridiculously low. You'll soon learn that balance isn't really my strongest skill. I pride myself on my business acumen, but I feel my best and closest to my true self when I get to flex my creative muscles. A day where I get to build a tabletop, digitally illustrate, sew, make resin coasters or stay up to the wee hours of the morning because I'm engrossed in a new art project is a good one for me.

In a couple of orbits around the sun I've transformed myself into a highly sought-after DJ, TV presenter, author, podcaster, entrepreneur, beauty influencer, professional opinion-haver and media personality, who sometimes has a nice amount of disposable income (which my mum thinks I should use to buy a house).

I do a lot of stuff because I want to, but most importantly because I can. It sounds strange, but the thing is, I grew up thinking that my quality of life would be perpetually limited by the fact that I wasn't rich, white, sporty, a man or a genius. I wasn't born into a lineage that would automatically guarantee me the best of everything, so therefore I was limited by what I could *actually* achieve. Coming from an immigrant, working-class, single-parent home, and not being particularly 'good' at anything, I'd been conditioned by society to think that it wouldn't be much. Through school I had standard test scores, and I almost failed my last year of high school because I 'never really applied myself' (as said by most of my teachers). I followed trends and latched onto anything that would bolster my identity. Wore what was appropriate, said what was expected, never dreamed too big because what's the point, right?

I don't have a sob story to share, don't stress. This is not a tale of how I overcame the most intense struggle to achieve absolutely rare and remarkable things, but I wanted to provide a bit of context on why I, of all people, am writing this book. It's not because I'm the most exceptional, or even the underdog, by any means. I'm just an ordinary girl who, through luck, skill, vision, determination and identifying my privilege, has transformed into someone who's achieved pretty extraordinary things (if I do say so myself). Of course, there are people who have done rarer and cooler things, but I'm not here to turn water into wine or pull a rabbit out of a hat. **I'm trying to debunk the theory that success is for the one per cent, those who have superhuman skills or have been lucky enough to be born into it.**

For the last five years, I've been a sponge, soaking up knowledge through experience, application and research. Trying to figure out how to cultivate and maintain a life worth living (by my own standards) — one that's exciting, enriching and not limiting. A life that gives me the ability to do and achieve way more than I, and others, expect of me.

And I think I've done it.

I mean, I'm literally writing a book (a professionally published, 'available in popular book retailers' book!) showing you how to achieve your own version of success, which is proof in itself. I created a formula that has helped me get what I want, kind of on my own terms. I have accomplished things I honestly never thought I could (or would), I prioritise my wants and needs, I have my dream jobs, I travel frequently, I have time to be creative, I've started multiple businesses, I can take time off work and, most importantly, I can nurture my mental health. I've got more emotional space to invest in my close relationships and to work on myself. I have disposable income. Heck, I even have savings! What I have might be the antithesis of what you want, but that doesn't matter.

The Success Experiment *exists to show you how to get whatever you want.*

You might be wondering why I want to tell you exactly how I did it all — it's not because I'm a virtuous saint who's desperate to pass on information that enables us all to collectively grow and thrive (though if that happens then yay!) — it's because I want to:

Prove that my success hasn't been a fluke

Recall and analyse what I did to get where I am

Encourage you to utilise some of my insights to achieve similar results

Reflect on what I could've done differently

Reflect on my relationship to success and how it has impacted my life, both positively and negatively

Use all my experiences from above, show you that there is a method that will get you closer to your end goal.

I called this book *The Success Experiment* because I've hypothesised that anyone who reads it, learns what I teach and then practises what they learn, will reach success. But, like any person, I have doubts. Yes, it worked for me, but I have wondered, is it all really as simple as following my advice?

It truly is! *The Success Experiment* is a self-help book, and by definition they provide resources and information designed to assist you in achieving things for yourself. These books are basically made to help you help yourself, which means that whether or not you see results is largely determined by the effort you put in. The information I share is only as helpful as you allow it to be. I'm not in the business of magic, and I can't make your biggest dreams come true by simply rubbing my belly. We've got to work together.

Reading this book won't fix every problem or grant every wish. It's just a couple of pieces of a huge jigsaw puzzle that's going to help you see your opportunities for success more clearly. In order for this experiment to work, you need to be open to what I'm teaching, and you have to be willing to make changes. **This book's ethos is: effort required, learning guaranteed, results preferred.**

Calling this an experiment, not a guide, allows me to be confident of my skills and the path I have taken to success, without pretending I have a supernatural ability to fix your life for you. What I won't do is overpromise and underdeliver.

Here's the thing, when I was living life and learning the lessons that I ended up recounting in this book, I had no idea I was on my way to this destination. Sure, I was into self-development — I actively tried to get smarter and work harder — but it wasn't like I knew a secret combination of actions to magically get me to this place. It was only when I reflected back on my journey to success that I was able to pick apart what choices had a major impact. Believe me when I say that this wasn't an easy or straightforward process. It was chaotic, confusing and difficult to analyse my subjective experiences objectively, because, of course, they're riddled with all kinds of personal biases. What combination of things worked because I'm me, and what things could others replicate for similar results?

Reflecting was kind of cathartic. Taking a trip down memory lane, trying to track my life in detail (when I was barely paying attention to all the details at the time) and getting to a point where I could confidently recall what worked and what didn't. Then — for your ease of consumption — I put that thang down, flipped it, reversed it. I figured out how to present everything in a linear, almost chronological way, then created a step-by-step system that you can reference for years to come. Don't let the sequential order of this book fool you, I was flailing about then, and I'm still flailing now. The key difference is that I've now experienced career and personal wins, which have made me less insecure about not always knowing the exact step to take and which remind me why it's important to try anyway.

My favourite thing about this experiment is that it's all about you — which, by proxy, means it's about me, too. It's about exploring what you can do, can't do, have to do and haven't done yet. It's about what you want and need (or think you want and need), and all the ways to get it. What we won't be focusing on is everything that impacts your life but can't be controlled. As much as I'd love to, there'll be no deep discussions about the patriarchy, glass ceilings, nepotism and the institutionalised education system. Not because they don't matter, because, believe me, I could talk all day about how much they do. It's because these external barriers are not my priority in this book. We can lament over them for a lifetime and still not be able to change these barriers in the ways we need to.

My plan is to show people that you don't have to be exceptional — or even the exception to the rule — to be successful. I've spent most of my working life (from the age of fifteen, whoa!) agonising over being more successful, without ever considering what success actually is. In my teens, I presumed that it was simply having a job while balancing school and a social life. In the earlier stages of adulthood, it was having multiple jobs in an effort to increase my chances of making heaps of money. The idea of balance I'd established in my school years had dropped off completely, and I found myself loving the idea of being a workhorse, finding gratification and validation in pushing myself to extremes with my workload. It wasn't enough just to drive myself into the ground doing stuff, I also wanted to make sure there were witnesses to my efforts.

A few things have changed since my adolescence. I'm still fascinated by the idea of personal value, increasing wealth, being 'successful' (on my own terms and by my own standards), self-actualisation, being a version of myself that I'm happy with and increasing my lust for life. But my personal markers of success have changed with time, so now my understanding has adapted to reflect this. I guess what I'm saying is that what I want has evolved not only because I have, but also because society has. As the world's standards change, it's pretty normal to absorb that on a personal level. Corporations are moving away from the forty-hour, five-day work week. More people are relocating from metropolitan areas to regional suburbs for a slower pace. Celebrities are less aspirational, as a new person gets cancelled every week for being racist, homophobic, bigoted, exploitative, or just generally (by the internet's standard) problematic. Billionaires are being called out for the insane amounts of wealth they hoard that could be redistributed to abolish poverty. It really be like that. Concepts and behaviour that we'd once considered 'normal' and ordinary are now being critiqued for the damage and harm they're doing. Capitalism, meat consumption, plastic use, fast fashion, the stupidly high cost of living, the exorbitantly high rates of burnout and exhaustion due to the average person spending approximately one third of their lives working, not to mention the steadily rising rates of mental health issues like anxiety, psychological distress and depression. **The bubble has burst, and many of us are divesting from everything we thought was right** (due to it being socially acceptable) to spend extra time figuring out what makes sense for us. At the point of writing this book, I'm able to tell you what I believe success is — but unfortunately the answer isn't as simple as I'd imagine you'd like it to be. The word itself can be really limiting and vague, because we default to conventional depictions of it. You know, suit and tie, marriage, kids and money. To me, it's about having the vision to want something that's truly aligned with you who are, coupled with the combination of trying, doing, learning and then applying your knowledge to reach your goal. Knowing what success is to you is one piece of the pie, but ultimately it needs to be measured by who you are and what you want, not by anybody else's arbitrary standards.

It's easy to conflate the process of trying and not achieving with failure. After all, it seems like our efforts should be met with a reward, right? If only life was that simple and fair. When we refuse to accept failure as a reality on the path to success, we allow apathy to drain us of our motivation to try again. We're often more concerned with how good it looks and feels to have more — stuff, friends, money, opportunities, experiences, positive emotions — than we did yesterday, instead of managing our own expectations about what the process will be like. We're dealing with a constant flurry of highs and lows, rather than working towards a less chaotic and more sustainable baseline of contentment.

How would our lives change if we spent more time identifying a few major milestones that we could work towards intentionally? How would our lives change if we weren't so scared to pursue what we actually wanted?

As someone who spends a lot of her time chasing instant-gratification, these are questions I ask myself often. It's like knowing that in a few months you want to travel, so instead of spending above your means every day on little things that make you feel good, you put aside a bit of money here and there so you can eventually book a flight and go. Vacation time!

My friend and podcast co-host Bobo said something to me once that really changed my life. She told me that humans are too caught up looking for symbols and depictions of happiness, rather than chasing actual happiness. **We are so distracted by the things we feel are supposed to enrich us, in a relentless pursuit to 'fulfil' ourselves by any means necessary, that we haven't even clocked that we might not be working towards what we truly want.** I can use this same analogy when it comes to goal setting.

'Trying' is the stage of getting your mind in order, preparing yourself to make an attempt or effort to do something; overthinking and analysing what's ahead of you until you can't anymore. Once you've theorised your master plan to death, told it to anyone who'll listen, and maxed out your Google tabs, it's time to start. When you begin, you won't just be attempting your plan once, but consistently. You'll do it over and over and over and over again, each time with effort and intention until you've fulfilled the brief, or at the very least, learned something during the process. How to do it, how not to do it, how to work differently or more efficiently — whatever it might be. Trying, doing and learning, done repetitively, all work to bring you closer to achievement. That process is the definition of success on which I have based this experiment.

In the time it takes you to read this book, you'll use a combination of what I did, what I wish I could've done, and what I learned, to find your own success. This experiment will ask you to try some things, do some things, learn some things, all of which will help you to achieve some things. You'll be given clear steps and tools that will show you how to get what you want from life, whether that's a new career, an improved mindset, fulfilling experiences, more money, or a greater understanding of yourself. In my personal success experiment I used some tools more than others, and as you progress you'll see that some things resonate with you more, but each exercise, concept and idea we learn along the way will be a cornerstone that you can return to. I'll try my hardest to omit vague anecdotes and confusing stories in favour of an interesting (but sometimes fallible) recollection of how I got to this point in my story, and explain how you can find success in your own story too. Because, in case you missed it, that's the whole point of this book. This is not another chance for you to fawn over someone else's story, wishing it was yours or resenting that it's not. I want you to read mine and find valuable lessons that apply to you.

My aim is to help you get what you want, so that at the end of this experiment you can say 'Wow, I really did that!'

This experiment is divided into six chapters:

Know who you are — In this chapter we're going to explore personality typing and learn how to use it as a tool for self-evaluation. This is where we'll figure out who you are, who you've been and how and why you're perceived in certain ways. Awareness is integral to success, as it helps you to understand what your strengths and weaknesses are.

Know who you want to be — Uncovering and accepting who you are through the self-evaluation tools we learn in the first chapter is an essential first step to self-development. In chapter two, we focus on the importance of honouring the person we want to be. This ideal person often isn't different from who you are now, but a dormant, undiscovered or aspirational version of yourself. It's the person you'd be if you learned to develop and harness the skills you already possess. Who are you on your best day? What would life be like if you were that person every day?

Know what you want — Who you are impacts what you want, and what you really, really want can often be tricky to figure out. Once you remove pressure from society, friends and family, what's left? Once you override your insecurities and turn your flaws into powers, what can you achieve? Chapter three is where we dig deep, set goals and discover this.

Know why you want it — Once we pass the halfway point in our experiment, it's time to do some heavy mental-lifting. You've figured out what you want, now you need to figure out why you want it. More specifically, what do you imagine achieving your goal will do for you? Will it make you happier? More secure? Braver? Bolder? Here's where you learn what motivates you, what moves you, and what's limiting you.

How you'll get it — The moment of truth. This chapter shows you how to combine introspection with action to get results. I'll be recalling all the tools I used over the last five years in detail, so you can start to tie together all the building blocks you've learned so far.

What will happen when you do — Success shouldn't be a fluke. This chapter is where we make sure whatever you've worked for sticks to you like polyester on sweaty skin.

Before we get into the experiment, I want to introduce you to some key themes, concepts and theories that have been lifesavers for me throughout my own success experiment.

SELF-ACTUALISATION
SELF-ACTUALISATION
SELF-ACTUALISATION
SELF-ACTUALISATION

If you have any interest in self-development, then I'd bet big bucks (gambling is toxic, so maybe don't do that) that you're also interested in being a self-actualised person. A self-actualised person is someone who understands how they come across, has realised who they are and what factors impact the way they act. They are (and feel!) fundamentally fulfilled because they are doing everything they believe they're capable of.

The trick to understanding what you're actually capable of is to first see yourself as who you truly are. In order to do this, you need to increase your level of self-awareness. I used to think being self-aware meant I just had to be conscious of what I was doing. Like, here I am purchasing another unnecessary piece of clothing, debating strangers on the internet or staying up to four am, again — but that's not really how it works.

Self-awareness is the ability to analyse yourself through both an objective and subjective point of view. You can improve this skill through personal reflection, introspection, evaluation and by observing how you think, what you think, how you feel and what's impacted that. **One of the hardest parts of self-awareness is realising it's impossible to know how many layers of ourselves we are yet to uncover.** That information could be exciting to some and spooky to others. It's also tricky to get to the crux of why we are the way we are, especially if you've never considered it before. What's influencing your personality, emotions, wants, habits, needs and flaws? Why do we do anything, fear some things and gravitate towards certain people?

It's one thing to remember who conventionally taught us stuff (parents, teachers, friends), but what about the stuff we soaked up like sponges just by existing? How do we get to the bottom of it? How will we ever really know how we're perceived? And how can we view ourselves through an objective lens when we're so subjectively biased? What do you do about personal blind spots? What if someone tells you that they perceive you a certain way, but you don't see it like they do? What happens when you discover your behaviours, mindsets or beliefs that you're not comfortable with? How do you change?

All questions that I can give you answers to in this book.

Throughout the experiment you'll find activities to accompany each new concept I teach you. These tests and activities are not scientific or clinical assessments, I'm not here to armchair-diagnose you. What they'll do is help you to apply what you've learned, give you some time to reflect on what resonates and what doesn't, and make sure that you continue the experiment equipped with new skills. Our first activity is a crash course in the basics of self-awareness. Think of this as a primer that will prepare you for the depths of your personality, which you'll unearth as we progress. The questions will ask you to assess and see yourself as others do, while simultaneously asking you to decipher the feelings and preconceived ideas you have towards certain traits. All of this will help you uncover the lens you use to view yourself and, by proxy, others.

Before you answer these questions, here are some tips to help you get the best results possible:

You only get out as much as you put in. It's a cliché, but clichés are generally true. The answers you write are meant to expose you — the more information you give, the more you have to analyse and draw conclusions from.

Write or type the list somewhere you can easily reference, whether that be a notebook, phone, a chalkboard in your bedroom or sticky notes on the fridge. This goes for all the activities in this experiment. It's really eye-opening to read back on answers years, months, weeks or even just a few days down the track, and see all the things that have changed and what's stayed the same.

Take your time. If an answer doesn't come to you straight away, don't move on. Wait, think and process until it does.

There is no right answer. Every activity is just for you, no one is going to cross-reference or check your answers, so there's no need to lie or pretend.

Like any good personality test, we're trying to discover what's beneath the surface.

Think of yourself like an iceberg: there are things about you which are obvious to everyone, and other parts that are below sea-level and yet to be discovered.

HOW TO BUILD SELF-AWARENESS FOR DUMMIES

1. **Make** two separate lists, one with all of your positive traits and one with the negatives. Look at your two lists and answer the following questions:

   a. What makes these traits positive or negative?
   b. When did you start to recognise these traits in yourself?
   c. Were these traits learned, and if so, where from?
   d. Are these traits often recognised in you by others?
   e. How does reading this list of traits make you feel?
   f. Have you always regarded the traits as good or bad, or has that changed with time?
   g. Do you recognise these traits in others?
   h. How do you regard other people with these traits?
   i. How do you feel about yourself when you speak to people with these traits?

2. **Did** you know that you have positive, negative and neutral traits that you're unaware of, but others can clearly see?

   a. How does this make you feel, and why?
   b. If you could adopt a new positive trait, what would it be?
   c. What would be the worst negative trait someone could say you have?

3. **How** we feel about ourselves and how we're perceived by others isn't always black and white. Although we may wish we could, most of us can't distil our personalities into neat boxes. Sometimes, we can't quite figure out why we feel the way we do about ourselves — why we're happy to be loud and boisterous in some environments, and a secretive recluse in others. Letting people really see you requires a level of vulnerability that needs to be trained and then affirmed by positive responses. **We're often afraid to show the world our full**

selves because we know we can't control the response we'll receive. Or maybe we simply don't like the feeling of being seen, flaws and all.

   a.   What are some behaviours or characteristics you have that people don't always see?
   b.   What are some behaviours or characteristics you like about yourself, but hide from others?
   c.   What are some behaviours or characteristics that you dislike about yourself and hide from others?
   d.   Why do you hide these traits, both the positive and negative?
   e.   What would encourage you to share these traits with others?

4. *Acknowledge* that you also have traits which are unclear to both you and others:
   a.   How does this make you feel?
   b.   Would you like to uncover these traits or not? Why?

Now that our first activity's done, how do you feel? It's a lot, right? Digging deep, unveiling relics and gems from the depths of your mind. Big archaeologist energy.

That whole exercise was devised to help provide you with deeper insight into how you see yourself and others, which ultimately works to improve your level of self-awareness. While self-analytical exercises like this may seem like simple tools, they provide heaps of useful information on how others see you and how we see ourselves in relation to them.

The concept of self-awareness is one that we'll keep coming back to throughout this experiment because it requires a lifetime of proactive and reactive learning. We naturally change over time — how we see ourselves, how we respond to things and our levels of openness will all ebb and flow. Traits you identify heavily with now might be traits that you leave in the dust as time goes on.

In my late teens and early twenties, I took pride in being loud-mouthed and obnoxious because I conflated shock-value with openness (I blame my copious reality-TV consumption). I thought success equalled celebrity, and the celebrities that were poppin' to me were popular due to their big personalities. As I've matured, I've settled into a quieter confidence. I value the validation and connection you get from being vulnerable, but also understand I don't have to share every part of myself with the world to be 'real' and authentic. I sometimes find myself wanting to slip back into the personality of my past because it's easy, but I stop myself because I know that not liking the person you portray to the outside world isn't a comfortable feeling. I just have to remind myself, *Lil, you won't die if you don't get the last word. You won't die if you don't have the coolest story. And your heart definitely won't stop if you don't boldly declare your two cents on every topic.*

If you feel like you're struggling to make progress on your development journey, don't worry, it happens. I feel most insecure about my growth when I'm comparing it to an arbitrary and often unattainable idea of what success looks like. Instead, measure your progress against the person you once were — it not only feels better, but is more practical and makes the changes easier to see. **Remember, being flawed is not the antithesis of developing as a person.** You'll probably notice that the more work you do to improve, the more you'll become privy to all the ways you weren't as developed as you thought. A renowned spiritual teacher named Jiddu Krishnamurti once said, 'The more you know yourself, the more clarity there is.' It's all part of the process. Just keep pressing on, moving forward and remember that learning about yourself is a big part of finding success.

When was the last time you thanked yourself for getting up in the morning? Congratulated yourself for handling conflict with grace? Commended yourself for following through with your commitments? That process is called self-celebration, and it's something you'll need to learn how to do if you plan to be more self-aware.

When it comes to any kind of success — relationship, career, lifestyle — I can have a very one-track mind. Eyes glued firmly to the prize, never stopping to revel in my little wins, or even take a break until I've accomplished what I set out to do. From experience, that's the easiest way to burn out.

When you don't take a moment to truly recognise you've done something awesome, a few things can happen:

You can subconsciously teach yourself that what you've achieved isn't important, which can decrease morale for future projects.

You can start to aim for stupidly grandiose goals, assuming that bigger goals are going to be more 'worth' the delayed gratification.

Or you can become too demotivated to put in the work because you haven't done anything proactive to acknowledge your efforts and boost your confidence.

Celebration is usually an indication of an accomplishment, and I can guarantee that there will be plenty of moments on your journey of getting what you want that are worthy of being recognised. Do you really want to internalise the feeling of not having achieved anything because you haven't taken a moment to reflect on all the good shit you've done?

Think about the kid who learns how to write their name for the first time. Does their teacher or parent dismiss their efforts because they can't spell complex words or string together grammatically correct sentences? No! They praise, uplift and reward them for their achievement because they can see that while it may not be the craziest feat for an adult, it's relatively huge for a kid. It's a milestone! All that positive reinforcement definitely affirms that the little one is on the right track and gives them more confidence to keep writing.

Instead of waiting until the end of the journey, find ways to highlight all the small things you've done well along the way.

Small wins relieve stress, inspire us and, most of all, contextualise our progress to date.

These celebrations act like a productivity fuel, giving you the juice you need to enthusiastically continue. Self-celebration is not about lying to yourself or building up your accomplishments to be greater than they are for a few feel-good points. It's also not about trying to prove to others that you're doing cool shit. **Self-celebration is a quiet confidence and inner knowledge that, when done correctly, can improve your drive, motivation and inspiration.** When done poorly, it can be interpreted as self-arrogance. Author and development coach Thomas J. Leonard said it best: 'Confidence is knowing exactly what you do well and don't do well; arrogance is a way to cover up what you don't do well.'

How should you self-celebrate? The long and short answer is do what works best for you, but a few basic tips include:

Recognise your daily wins. Identify small moments in the day to reflect on things you've done well. They could be as simple as waking up on time, getting all your emails answered or cooking yourself a fresh and nutritious dinner. You don't need to throw yourself a party every time you tick something off the to-do list but pausing to give yourself some mental props is more than enough. You could even spend a few minutes writing down everything you accomplished so you can visibly see it all.

Tell someone who gets it. I don't know about you, but I can be really secretive about the good stuff that's happened to me because I'm concerned that it can be perceived as bragging, or I simply don't think the person will truly understand why I'm so hyped. Mentally sift through your list of close friends, colleagues or loved ones who can really comprehend the significance of what you've done, or even just find someone who's a great listener. Either way, stop hoarding your good news.

Develop a sense of gratitude for basic things. Sounds simple, but it's hard. We live in a world that profits off our insecurities by instilling a sense of 'lack'. We're constantly reminded of all the things we don't have, all the reasons we're not perfect and all the ways these are going to impact our ability to ever truly be satisfied. The easiest way to combat this is to write down (first daily, and then at random moments when you need a boost) all the small things that have made your day liveable. The fact that you had money to eat, a phone to entertain yourself, friends to laugh with, toilet paper at your disposal, a pen with ink and a car with petrol. Having all these things readily available, although expected, really does make the difference between a shitty day and an amazing one. Take it in. Smell the roses! It's so awesome.

Treat yourself to physical rewards (mental kudos doesn't always hit the spot!). This one's pretty self-explanatory, but it's for the people who need a little more than verbal validation, the folks who want tangible representations for their efforts. I don't advocate spending above your means as a reward for doing stuff, but I definitely think you could allocate a teensy budget to treat yourself.

Reflect on past achievements. Sit down somewhere quiet, close your eyes and try to recall a time when you did something great by your own standards. Something that made you feel good, proud and accomplished. Something that didn't need to be validated by others for you to acknowledge its importance. Compare your feelings about it from then until now. How did you conquer it? Did you spend enough time celebrating yourself?

Learning how to appreciate yourself is a skill that requires effort and repetition to master. It can feel weird to start, but trust me, you shouldn't wait until you've reached your goals to be proud of yourself.

Big goals can take a long time to achieve, and there'll be a lot of little wins (and lessons learned) along the way, so why put off feeling good?

You can practise self-celebration as part of a morning ritual, or my preference is to draw on it whenever you feel yourself descending into a pit of self-doubt.

THE REAL YOU IS SIMPLY A METAPHORICAL FOSSIL WAITING TO BE REVEALED THROUGH introspection.

CRITICAL THINKING

Critical thinking is the ability to rationally and objectively analyse information, separating yourself and your biases, and allowing yourself to look at a situation more accurately.

Being a 'good' critical thinker allows you to make reasonable judgements that are logical, nuanced and well thought-out, instead of jumping to conclusions on everything based on your own experiences. This way of thinking helps you to make more effective decisions and understand yourself and others better.

On a small level, you think critically every day, so don't be confused or overwhelmed — this isn't actually a new concept. Every time you consciously and deliberately choose what to eat, how to get to work, what words to use when diffusing an argument with a friend, you're thinking critically. **It's the process of weighing your options, thinking about the impact of each and acting accordingly.** To consciously think more critically when considering new information, there are a few questions you can ask yourself:

What am I looking at?

What is this information actually saying?

What information is needed to help me understand it better?

Why is this information important?

Who is impacted by this information?

Who is giving me this information, and is it biased?

Why should I listen to this person?

How do I know that this information is true?

What can I learn from this?

Imagine analysing this book using those questions as a guide. You now have to consider my perspective and how my own personal experiences and biases are skewing the information I'm giving you. What privileges do I have that can make life easier for me and harder for you? What resources do I have access to that make dreaming big a reasonable thing to do? How does my lived experience make me a credible source of information?

Suddenly this process is not just as simple as you reading a book about success. Everything I write, every lesson I recount, every anecdote I share is filtered through my own individual way of viewing the world. In the same way that how you respond to this book is going to be heavily impacted by your mindset, and how receptive you are to the information I'm sharing. I'm telling you this because it's so vital to have a healthy level of scepticism. **Be discerning about what you read and what conclusions you draw.**

Now that you're thinking critically, questioning my motivations, trustworthiness and the stuff I'm sharing, use that same curiosity to research, learn more about who I am, what I'm teaching you and make your own judgements accordingly.

Critical thinking effectively means that we avoid taking things at face value. After all, face value can often be a reflection of our biased past experience, or the ways in which we've been programmed by society, family or friends to view the world around us.

When I was a teen I loved drinking Powerade, not necessarily to replace lost electrolytes, but I liked the taste and it was always available at my local 7-Eleven. If you're familiar with the drink, you know it comes in every colour of the rainbow (all of which I happily drank), but my mum would always fuss when I bought the blue flavour. From memory, she said that we shouldn't drink blue drinks because cleaning products are blue, and so the visual always made her uncomfortable. She stressed to me that it would be 'safer' to drink the other colours. I doubt she really thought that Powerade would switch out the contents of the bottle to Windex, but Mum had clearly seen enough cleaning products to now associate the blue liquid with poison.

How we view the people around us, the world and our experiences in it is informed by our personal bias. Our preconceived ideas are not always wrong, but they can be misleading. It's easy to forget that's how the other seven billion people on the planet think too. As obvious as it sounds, you'd be surprised by the amount of people who govern themselves with only their own bias, considering nothing more than how they view the situation at hand.

Applying a critical lens to our experiences reminds us that outcomes, and how we view them, can be limitless.

While discerning sports drinks from cleaning products may not be your main reason for learning how to critically think, this practice will help you cultivate a huge catalogue of new abilities, like open-mindedness, self-reflection, logical and analytical thinking, self-evaluation, reasoning, confidence in debating and the ability to question. Critical thinking is a skill for life. It reminds you that all the barriers (physical, mental, spiritual and emotional) you come across, both in this experiment and life after, won't always have a formulaic step-by-step response, but by thinking critically you can find a way to prepare yourself, anyway. It's the ultimate troubleshooting skill.

As you learn to discover what you want, it's really important to look at these things with a critical lens. Give yourself space and time to evaluate your life, problems, goals, issues, and form clear judgements, based not only on your experience and your intuition, but on an objective analysis of the information. Once those judgements are formed, they need to be re-evaluated again and again and again until you're in a position where you feel like you've considered all options — that's when you act. You might not feel certain of your decision forever; one day you might be all in and the next day you might pivot and do a one-eighty. That's OK, it means you're still thinking. You can always re-evaluate after you've made a choice, that's the beauty of it. The timeline for how often you need to evaluate is something you will learn to assess on a case-by-case basis. Like most fulfilling activities, critical thinking is a process, and luckily for you, this process can be taught.

How would our lives change if we set goals based on what would truly make us fulfilled,

rather than what was easiest or felt the most accessible?

HOW TO

CRITICALLY THINK

SLIGHTLY BETTER

Critical thinking is the skill that's going to underpin every concept in this book, so it's vital that you grasp the concept of it in order to start practising.

TIP ONE: Channel your inner toddler and ask 'why' to absolutely everything.

Toddlers are the original critical thinkers; their curiosity and desire to understand can trump their need to act with blind confidence. Question your beliefs, wants, likes, dislikes. Question others and then cross-reference this information with your own understanding. See where your thinking intersects and where it doesn't. You're not questioning to dispute, but merely gathering all the information you can.

If questioning is too broad of a directive, try the classic who, what, why, when, where, how technique as a starting point. Here's an example:

Scenario: I want to buy a new car.

Why do you want to buy a new car?

Who has influenced you wanting to buy a car?

Who are you going to buy the car from?

What car do you want, and how did you come to that decision?

What are your non-negotiables for the car's specs?

When do you want to buy the car?

How are you going to buy a new car; ie, can you afford to buy a car?

Through answering those questions, you can create a framework around buying a car, which will give you the information you need to make a more considered purchase. The statement 'I want to buy a car' suddenly transforms into 'I want to buy a Nissan Cube that's between ten and fifteen years old with an automatic transmission. I don't want to spend more than ten thousand dollars, which I know is a standard price for this car due to my research. I don't want to buy a new car because I watched a video online that says cars depreciate in value as soon as you drive them off the lot, and with that in mind I would like my car to be used with minimal signs of wear.' Do you see the difference?

TIP TWO: Get comfortable with not always looking smart.

There's a certain humility attached to learning; you can never be too cool to know better. Asking 'why', especially through childhood, can be interpreted as 'you don't know because you're dumb', as opposed to 'you don't know because you haven't accessed this information yet'.

Here's a challenge for you. Sometime this month, I want you to engage in a conversation you don't feel smart enough to have. Not because I want you to make a fool of yourself, but because it's important to practise thinking (read: properly using your brain) rather than answering questions reflexively or excluding yourself from certain environments. Take it as an opportunity to learn, explore further concepts you don't really get and expand your mind, rather than letting insecurity lead. Don't limit yourself to topics you know back to front, or environments that don't foster excellence. **One hard conversation a day keeps a limiting worldview at bay.** Here are some phrases that can help:

'I don't understand, could you please clarify?'

'I've never considered that perspective before, could you please elaborate?'

'Where can I learn more about this?'

'Could you please explain that slightly differently?'

TIP THREE: Try a bite-sized approach to complex issues, and break them down into smaller, more digestible pieces.

Start solving the teensy-weensy problems first and combine all the answers to highlight a common thread, which will help you to figure out the bigger issue.

Example: You work in a full-time role as a social-media manager. You know you're good at your job because you've had awesome feedback from your boss, yet it's been more than a year and you haven't received a pay rise or promotion.

Your response: My boss dislikes me and is lying when they tell me I'm good at my job. I'm not an asset to the company and that's why I've haven't been promoted ... I haven't been fired because they can't find a reason to do so without telling me how they really feel about me.

What's wrong with that response? Depending on how you frame it, there's technically nothing wrong with thinking like that, as your perception is valid. However, if we applied some critical thinking skills to that situation, we may find a different solution.

First, let's question the issue:

How do you know you're good at your job?

Why do you want a promotion?

What will happen when you get a promotion?

How will you respond if your boss doesn't want to give you a promotion?

Does your boss know you want a promotion?

Has your boss provided you feedback that confirms you have some work to do to become better at your job?

Have your colleagues received pay rises or promotions and, if so, what steps did they take to attain them?

Is there room for growth in your role?

Have you advocated for yourself and spoken to your boss about a promotion?

If we answer these questions with the knowledge we have and seek out information for the answers we don't, we suddenly have a much clearer picture. You can use this type of inquisitive technique for any old scenario. Then break down the responses into even smaller pieces based on facts, instead of projecting how you feel onto the situation first. Your feelings matter, but **when critically thinking we have to prioritise what we know over what we assume**. This scenario is the perfect example of what can happen when you choose your bias over the information provided, which can then cause you to catastrophise.

CATASTROPHISE:

Catastrophising is to assume the worst has happened or will. Often, catastrophising can involve believing that you're in a worse situation than you really are or exaggerating the difficulties you face.

CONFIRMATION BIAS:

This bias refers to the ways in which people look for evidence that supports their own opinions, rather than looking at the whole picture. It leads to selective observation, meaning you overlook other (often important) information and instead focus on things that fit your view. You may even reject new information that contradicts your initial beliefs.

TASK

Using the three tips for critical thinking, try to analyse the hypothetical (although completely possible) workplace example we discussed previously. Once you've done that, answer the questions below:

1. What questions would you ask to help this person critically unpack their situation?

2. Did thinking critically change your perspective on this scenario? If so, how?

3. What are the easiest and hardest things about critical thinking?

4. What difference do you think critically thinking can make in your life?

Evaluating yourself immediately after learning the concept of critical thinking seems premature, and I want to give you the chance to become competent in your new skill before trying it on the biggest tasks. Part of being confident in your critical-thinking ability means being aware of the areas that come naturally to you and those that don't. As you develop your skills in this area, you should find it easier to:

Figure out if there are any inconsistencies between how you view yourself or your situation. You'll be more aware of how your mindset does or doesn't match your actions. You'll learn how to see yourself as you really are (flaws and all) rather than in an idealised way. You'll learn how to be gentle with yourself when you notice areas for growth. This is a good way to take accountability for the positive and negative stuff that happens to you.

Find your own consistent approach to problem solving. You'll be doing a lot of it in this book and throughout your lifetime, so it's vital you develop a formula that you can tweak and adjust early, rather than when you're in the midst of a dilemma.

Reflect on how you see the world, in addition to what informs your beliefs and behaviour. When you're able to dissect ideas it's easier to connect dots to figure out why things are the way they are.

MANIFESTATION

and the law of attraction

A buzzword of sorts, manifesting has become synonymous with the idea of wishing things into existence. The perception is that if you think super hard, reality will buckle under the pressure of your desperation and give you what you want. From my understanding, the concept of manifesting and the law of attraction was popularised by Oprah after she promoted the self-help book *The Secret* by Rhonda Byrne. Oprah said *The Secret* highlighted a message she'd been trying to share with the world for decades. The book claims that what you think, and how you think it, can change your life. In summary, the author says that if you follow the philosophy of *The Secret*, you can create the life you want — whether that means getting out of debt, finding a more fulfilling job or even falling in love. To date, the book has sold over thirty million copies worldwide, and has been translated into fifty languages. It's safe to say it was, and still is, a pop-culture phenomenon. I skim-read the book in high school, took what resonated with me (the get-stuff-quick approach) and left what didn't.

The Secret and its themes are extremely polarising. Many people approach it with scepticism and distrust, because to them the practice can sound vague and witchy. We've all thought about winning a million dollars or sleeping with celebrities (just me?) and that hasn't happened for the majority of us ... There are people who feel empowered by the thought of being able to change their own circumstances for the better, and then there are those with a fair few criticisms on whether it actually works and how. Is manifesting a superpower, magic or scientifically viable? If people can really change their situation with nothing more than their mind, are they also to blame for all the bad stuff that happens to them? What about the people born into extreme poverty or sickness? Or those born into wealth and privilege?

I believe that we live simultaneously between two worlds, an inner and outer, both as real as the other. There's the main outer world, which contains the amalgamated experiences of a couple of billion people. It's the one where societal norms, convention and collective truth exists. The place where people are expected to go to school, enter the workforce, get married, tell the truth, be personable, live and die. The one where we just know that the sky is blue, the grass is green, the Earth is round, the sun is hot and drinking eight glasses of water a day is vital for good health. In this place, there are common ideas that are shared, generally accepted and often not disputed. In this place, you are one of many, working in tandem with everyone else to keep the cogs of the machine moving.

In addition to that outer world, I think that every single person has their own individual and unique inner world. A personal reality created by your perception. A place that moves, warps and changes based on your feelings, beliefs and experiences. A place where *your* truth can often supersede *the* truth. In other words, what we think is real is what's real to us. It's simply how we've interpreted what reality should be, based on our own idea of what we've been shown.

This inner world is not necessarily separate from the real, outer world, and it's not a physical place that you can go to — it's what's going on in your mind. The two worlds go hand in hand. If the outer shows you what is there, what is generally accepted and what is 'real', the inner is how you personally process and perceive these things. It's almost as if you are the centre of the world and everything orbits around you. As you increase your understanding of yourself and your surroundings you start to interpret what you see, what you hear and what happens to you based on how you feel about it. Naturally, you start to measure everything around you based on your internal metric-system. But, interestingly enough, what you think is real isn't necessarily factual. That's not a bad thing, it's just the result of being a sentient being.

Perhaps your outer world tells you that, because you graduated high school with poor results, your career choices are now limited. But in your inner world, you have curated a sense of imagination where you believe that you can rise above your circumstances, upskill, learn and network to reach the goal that others think you're not in the right league for.

In theory, every person has the capacity to see the world in the same way but because our personal experiences skew what we see, we can experience the same thing completely differently. Our memory, our inability to recall information correctly, our preferences, our past, our fears, our biases and our wants all impact how we perceive our reality. Certain environments, situations and even people can trigger you to interpret anything through a more positive or negative lens.

EVERYTHING YOU SEE, TOUCH, TASTE, HEAR, & FEEL IS SPECIFIC TO YOU.

The point is, once you realise that your reality is tailored to you, by you, you can begin to take more accountability for what has and hasn't, will and won't happen to you. Have you ever heard of the phrase 'You're the master of your own universe?' This is exactly what it's referring to; people aren't saying that you have the ability to magic good stuff into your life because you want it, but you aren't as limited by reality as you think, because in some ways, you technically control your own reality. This is the foundation of manifesting.

I've always considered myself to be a spiritual-ish person. Being raised Christian (then opting out of organised religion) will do that to you. I was introduced to the concept of prayer as a child, which kind of put manifesting into perspective for me as an adult because there are heaps of overlapping themes, like speaking things into existence, knowing that your thoughts can impact what does or doesn't happen to you, and understanding that language needs to be specific so that the outcome of your prayers are aligned with what you actually want. I was also trained to be mindful of what I thought and said out loud, because someone (God) was listening and would strike me down if I was thinking naughty, hateful or rude things. In hindsight, the whole thing just felt like a positive mental exercise — a safe place and a cathartic experience that often resulted in clarity or a renewed belief that what you desired was on its way to you.

The question of whether manifesting actually works reminds me of how I approached prayer based on what I was taught (and how I understood it). It wasn't about making a wish and adding it to God's to-do list, but knowing that someone, somewhere, who potentially had power, was listening. And it was my job to frame my request in a way that was direct and concise, so if perhaps this almighty, omnipotent figure suddenly stumbled across my prayer (and was feeling charitable), the outcome would be perfect. I distinctly remember prayer being regarded as a meditation of sorts, a time to quiet your mind, zone in to solve your own problems. A time to let God (or your intuition), guide you into an answer, rather than sitting idly by hoping that your time will come. Not disputing that the Big Guy didn't have our back, but that he (she or they) was more interested in working together. If your prayers are never seen or answered, you'd still be taking strides in the right direction.

The concept of manifesting was reintroduced to me when I was finally making enough income from DJing that I quit my full-time-turned-part-time job in PR, social media and digital communications, and tried my hand at TV presenting. I know, it's a lot to wrap your head around but bear with me. I didn't have any experience at all, but I did have a bit of an ego after turning my lacklustre working life into an enviable one. My career in PR had me feeling like a useless fish out of water. It wasn't that I was bad at my job, it was just that my expectations of what the job would entail didn't match the reality. The only reason I'd started working in that industry was because I'd binge-watched MTV's *The Hills* as a teen, and thought it looked cool to dress up for work and rub shoulders with 'the elite'. The reality was that ninety-seven per cent of the job was selling a product I didn't care about, working hard with little recognition and feeling like every project required me to give twenty-seven hours a day and my firstborn child. I guess I was most worried that I would physically burn out before I'd be able to proactively change careers. That I'd be so emotionally exhausted I would be resigned to my situation, staying in an environment that robbed me of my joy because I'd inevitably lose the will to try. I needed to move on to something more fulfilling, especially while I had a couple drops of drive left.

I can't really recall what made me turn my sights back to manifesting. Perhaps it's the fact that I'd been hardwired to turn to spirituality in times of complete despair, and because prayer didn't feel like an option, maybe my brain connected the dots and took me back to *The Secret*. Another skim-read later — this time with an adult lens and the experience my career so far had given me — and I could confirm there were themes that continued to resonate with me, like the importance of gratitude, optimism, clear visualisation and the power of shifting your perspective to positively impact your mindset.

But there were still elements of *The Secret* that didn't land. Firstly,

The Secret tells you that the path to getting what you want can be broken down into a three-step process: ask, believe and receive. These steps are based on a quote from the Bible, Matthew 21:22, 'And all things, whatsoever ye shall ask in prayer, believing, ye shall receive.' I can't lie, I loved the way that sounded, but given I desperately needed an out from my job, I wasn't inspired by the idea of opening my heart to the possibilities and waiting patiently for results. I needed a more proactive and pragmatic strategy that gave me agency. I read reviews on *The Secret* to get a vibe of what other people thought about it. That research spiral resulted in a few keywords typed incessantly into Google: *manifestation, the law of attraction* and *the New Thought movement*. Up until that point, I had thought manifestation was just the name of Byrne's method. It hadn't occurred to me that there would be different approaches to the practice — in hindsight, duh, of course there would be! I started opening up tabs and got acquainted with these ideas, but none of them really resonated.

My manifestation method started as an amalgamation of things the internet told me to do that didn't actually stick with me. Fake it till you make it, they recommended. So I pushed through all the discomfort and alarm bells that told me I was a phony who was wasting her time, because I didn't want that to be the truth. Granted, I didn't know if I was hocus-pocusing my life away, in the same way that I couldn't guarantee that it wasn't not working.

It took me too many years of roleplay-manifesting and looking at strangers on the internet for a step-by-step practice I could imitate, only to realise that there is literally no one-size approach to betterment. **Most things that involve improving a unique individual will require a unique and individual approach.** I usually know this like the back of my hand, but when I was feeling insecure and my self-esteem was shaken up I didn't trust myself or my intuition to get me out of the situation.

For this same reason, manifesting isn't really something you can 'teach' but it's a skill that can be refined using my framework. I will show you what I do, but just know that you'll have to cobble up a method that works best for you.

Disclaimer: My intention isn't to invalidate alternate methods. My approach to manifesting isn't better or worse than any other, it's just different, and it's what works for me. I also don't attribute manifesting as the only way to get what I want or my preferred way to achieve my goals — I use it in conjunction with everything else I show you in this book. Like every other tool I share, it's a suggested approach, not a mandatory one. If you like it, use it; if you don't, then don't.

WHAT IS MANIFESTING?

I define manifesting as the act of willing positive or negative results into existence through belief, intent and action. Manifesting is the practice of shifting your thoughts to change your perception of the world and your experience in it.

WHY WOULD SOMEONE NEED TO MANIFEST?

I wouldn't categorise it as a need, but if the idea is something you connect with, I'd recommend using it when you feel you've become a passive character in your own story. For the times you feel like life is just happening to you and you have little control of your own experiences. For the times you're just existing and feel like you'd benefit from captaining your own ship and steering for a little while. It's ideal for people who want to proactively change their behaviour and mindset in the hopes of improving their situation.

WHAT IS THE LAW OF ATTRACTION?

The law of attraction is the belief (whereas manifesting is the action) that positive or negative thoughts will bring positive or negative experiences into a person's life.

These ideas might already mirror your approach to living or you might be confused as heck by the idea that your thoughts could shape your experiences and perceptions; all working to make your dreams come true. It's OK, we're all learning here, and these new concepts can be a lot to take in at first. So, before we move on, I have to make three quick disclaimers about manifesting:

1. *You don't* have to be spiritual, wiccan, pagan, or blessed with supernatural gifts to manifest.

2. *Manifesting isn't* necessarily linear, as in 'I want this thing, and now it's mine'. The idea is that you do as much work as necessary to get to your goal. You need to understand that there is going to be a number of external aspects that might inhibit you, but you actually don't have enough hours in the day to focus on the things that are out of your control.

3. *Manifesting is* not a new or rare concept. You're always manifesting; you just have to learn how to harness it. Your mind is constantly churning, thinking and orbiting around something. Your job is to focus on what's in your head and understand that a big part of what's happening in there is affecting what happens on the outside.

When I started diving into my manifesting research, I came across the theory that our brains can't tell the difference between reality and fantasy. I was immediately hooked. Neuroscientist Anil Seth has a really great TED Talk about this, where he says that 'We're all hallucinating all the time, including right now; when we agree about our hallucinations, we call it "reality".' With that in mind, thinking your way into a better result doesn't seem so far-fetched, right? However, there's a still a crucial element of manifesting we have to discuss.

Imagine this: you're faced with a situation that fuels your insecurities. Maybe you'd thought that by this age you would have travelled more or have a better job and more fulfilling relationships. Maybe there was a time you weren't impacted by these looming life-deadlines, but as you've gotten older you've begun to feel a sense of pressure from yourself and those around you. You might have been optimistic in the past, but with no noticeable results, your coping mechanism is now anticipating the worst rather than hoping for the best. Regardless of the reality of your situation (your outer world), your brain (your inner world) is probably already processing fear, failure, stress and a ton of other shitty emotions. From there, your very capable brain is scanning these less-than-ideal thought patterns and storing them in your mind, forever associating these feelings with this insecurity-fuelling situation.

Because you haven't seen the amazing results you'd hoped for, it becomes easy to start processing trying as failing. Eventually, you stop trying altogether, which I personally think is just a more potent form of failing. Imagine if from the beginning you were able to keep an open mind, aware of your options but choosing to prioritise thoughts that keep you on course.

We never know when we're moments away from our big break, so I think it's vital to keep your eyes on the prize — that way, when the situation reveals itself, you're ready to respond.

How do I

A simple question with a not-so-simple answer. Before I had fully conceptualised my idea for *The Success Experiment* my plan was to actually write a book about manifesting. In 2019 I'd self-published an e-book that shared my simple approach to it, which then was found by my amazing publisher, Pantera Press, which brings us to the present day. I initially thought I was writing a pretty one-size-fits-all guide on how to change your life by learning a very specific skill, but it quickly became a greater discussion on how the skill wouldn't even work if you didn't first assess all the other things impacting your ability to achieve.

You see, the framework for my manifestation guide was simple to me. Three concise steps: belief, intent, and action.

BELIEF

Believe you can actually accomplish this thing you want so badly. A lack of belief fosters insecurity and doubt, which eventually causes inaction.

INTENT

Figure out why you actually want this thing. What do you envision it's going to do for you? How do you imagine it's going to improve your life? Knowing what motivates you means that when barriers come up, you have a better idea of how to overcome them.

ACTION

The vital missing step in a lot of the manifestation methods I'd researched. Most of them covered why mindset was valuable, but very few stressed that in order to achieve, you actually have to apply yourself.

MANIFEST?

However, just as I'd critiqued the manifesting methods I researched, I started to pull apart mine. Those three steps alone were definitely showing people what they needed to do, but not how it needed to be done or even why. In exploring and dissecting each priority, I realised that there had to be an emphasis on self-development, evaluation, exploration and critical thinking. Without that, I was just another vague approach to wishful thinking.

Those three steps are still the bones and the structure of this book, however the elaboration is what transforms this from 'a book about manifesting' to a self-development book rooted in manifestation principles, but strengthened with a ton of other practical solutions.

Section One

(steps one and two) of this book is all about self-belief and how that impacts your ability to achieve.

Section Two

(steps three and four) of this book is all about getting to the core of what you want and why you want it, which is essentially uncovering your intention.

Section Three

(steps five and six) of this book is all about figuring out what exactly needs to be done and how to do it. This is action.

Keep reading, absorbing and applying and by the end of the book, you'll have learned to manifest.

REFLECTION
REFLECTION
REFLECTION
REFLECTION

The journey to acquiring the thing you want isn't linear. The plans you set to reach your goal are unlikely to happen in the ways you expect. But isn't that just how life is? If we stopped wanting things just because there was a chance that we wouldn't get them, then I guarantee our lives would be bland, dull and lacklustre. Self-awareness reminds us that we have to shatter the delusions created by our expectations and remember that a lot of those expectations come from the ways we've been conditioned by society. Our plans and ideas constantly change, often due to forces outside our control, so the best we can do is **stay aware, adapt and reflect on what's happening around us and what we can learn from it.**

It's easy to get so caught up in the acts of doing, moving forward, accelerating and progressing that we forget to pause and assess what we've been through and how that impacts our future. Taking time to think is extremely helpful in getting a better grasp on who you are and your situation.

This is why it's vital that you keep checking back in with yourself and your plan; amending your strategy and expectations accordingly. Like any skill, learning how to reflect takes time and if you've never really done it before, it can feel like you're obsessing over the past. Here are some questions to get you into a reflection mindset:

How would you describe yourself to someone who doesn't know you?

What qualities are you most proud of? Which are you uncomfortable with?

What are you most grateful for?

Who are the people you spend the most time with and why?

What are the biggest life lessons you've learned and what have they taught you about yourself?

When do you feel most like yourself?

How did it feel to answer those questions? It's normal to talk about yourself, but to analyse is a whole different ballpark. There's no right answer. It's important that you focus on purging all the information you have; doing so will allow you to assess, analyse and draw the best conclusions for yourself.

As you progress through this experiment, you'll be doing some deep analysis into who you are, what you want and why you want it. All of this is a lot to process, so if at any point you start feeling off-kilter, you can check back in by asking yourself :

How do I feel about my goals; are they clear and defined? Do I feel motivated to pursue them?

Are these feelings better or worse than when I began this experiment? Why?

Does my plan need to evolve in any way? If so, how?

KNOWING YOUR STRENGTHS IS JUST AS IMPORTANT AS KNOWING YOUR WEAKNESSES, AND YOU NEED THEM BOTH TO CREATE A FRAMEWORK FOR SUCCESS.

Section One

STEP ONE

Chapter One:
*Know Who
You Are*

STEP TWO

Chapter Two:
*Know Who You Want
to Be*

STEP ONE

Know  *you*

CHAPTER ONE

who are

WHAT THIS CHAPTER *WILL* TEACH YOU

How to unpack your personality, behaviour and motivations, to discover who you really are

How to self-evaluate and discover ways you can improve, by your own standards

What your strengths are and how you can use them to your advantage

What personality tests are and why you should do them

How to conquer your Achilles heel

How to view yourself through a critical lens

ONE

WHAT THIS CHAPTER *WON'T* TEACH YOU

How to stay the same person forever

How to avoid abundance and good luck

How to stay stagnant while avoiding growth and personal evolution

How to pretend that you don't have flaws

How to hide parts of yourself in the hopes of appearing 'perfect'

Who are you?
Who are you?
Who are you?
Who are you?

That's a loaded question, and depending on how you read it, where you put the intonation and inflection, your response could be wildly different. For this first chapter, I want to get to know *you*.

I want to give you room to reintroduce yourself to yourself. I feel like we often go through life on autopilot; acting the way we've always done because it's familiar, thinking the way we always have because we haven't had time to check if our perspective has changed. I get it, life is a lot. There are so many distractions and things to keep us stimulated.

Every day I learn more and more about who I am, but as the saying goes 'the more you know, the more you realise you don't know'. Usually that quote is in reference to concepts, not self, but I find it can be applied to both. Some days I like egg yolks, some days I don't. Sometimes I swear up and down that I'm a textbook extrovert, then I spend the next five days dodging plans like the plague. If I'm aware of these things, then maybe I really do know myself and inconsistency is part of my brand. Or maybe I'm constantly evolving as a person, and instead of letting myself be, I'm trying to force myself to be decisive about everything. **The point is, being a human is all about being fluid: transforming and evolving based on our experiences.**

Even so, we are viewed differently based on who's looking at us.

I'm someone's daughter, sister, best friend, worst enemy, aspiration and inspiration; being any one of those things doesn't negate another. They're all me. But as I write this, it's occurred to me that you don't actually know who I am, so let me properly introduce myself.

As you know, my name is Lillian. At the time of writing this book, I'm a 25-year-old Ghanaian-Australian woman with an Aries Sun, Aquarius Moon and Pisces Rising.

For as long as I can remember, I've been inundated with conversations about identity and how my own would impact my life experience. Dressing myself in a way that has been described as *extra*, *a lot*, *over-the-top*, *gaudy*, *excessive*, *extreme* and *costumey*, coupled with the intersectionality of being black AND a woman and all the stereotypes that come with that, my body throughout my life has been inherently politicised. From a time when I was a plaid-donning, platform-wearing, side-fringe-having scene-teenager; or more recently when I wore rainbow-coloured wigs daily because I was preoccupied with being unique (it's my Aquarius Moon, I swear). How I look has always been a topic of discussion.

At one point I thought being noticed was the height of flattery, so striving to be as highly visible (socially and aesthetically) became part of my identity. Finding ways to be noticed, ogled and stared at was my priority. In retrospect, I think I internalised being a spectacle and, in some way, believed that how I looked was the most important thing about me. **But then it dawned on me — what people see doesn't actually say much about who I am.** I had this realisation when people began attributing traits to me based on my appearance. They'd assume things like:

You're black so you must not be Australian.

You're African so you must not speak English.

You're confident so you must not have insecurities.

You wear bright colours, so you obviously want to be ogled.

You're sexually literate so you must be promiscuous.

You're overweight so you must be unhealthy (OK, I can't dispute that one; my diet is shocking).

Naturally, I felt misunderstood and began to feel like people weren't seeing the real me. I developed a chip on my shoulder; thinking that people not interpreting me the same way I saw myself meant the world was out to get me. Didn't they see I had interests? A personality? Hobbies? The short answer is no, and that's because I spent little time communicating these parts of myself to the outside world. Upon further reflection, I started to question what these interests I thought I had even were ... Were they mine, or did I simply inherit them from my friends and family? I began to ask myself: what do I care about? What do I like about myself? What am I good at?

Unsurprisingly this sent me spiralling, and instead of exploring these uncomfortable questions further, I kept changing the way I looked, hoping it would magically give me insight into who I really was. I dressed like a pop-punk fanatic, a fancy mum, a club kid, a cool aunty in kaftans, a quirky-yet-edgy librarian; fast-forward to now, where I feel like I'm an amalgamation of all of my style-personas. **Adulthood showed me that how you look is vital to how you're perceived by those around you, but your values, point of view, experiences and personality say a hell of a lot as well.** This chapter is where we uncover what these values are and learn how to express them effectively and authentically.

The journey to discovering who I was — aside from the way I looked — started by accident. In high school I was obsessed with personality tests, but I only thought of them as novel activities for lunchtime.

I hadn't yet considered that these tests could be helpful self-discovery tools. Personality tests are a simple way to dissect yourself through asking introspective questions like: do you prefer time alone or with others? Do you prefer concrete plans or spontaneity? Some questions are multiple choice, while others are on a spectrum. Once you're done, you'll receive a summary that reflects what you chose, providing insight into how those responses impact the way you act.

Fast-forward to when I was nineteen years old. I was studying fashion business because I liked clothes and presumed that meant I'd also love the industry. Not quite ... I was distracted in class and wasn't getting any work done, so I decided to go to the library afterwards to catch up (roleplay academia). On my first and only visit, I ended up getting a phone call from a friend, which both defeated the purpose of taking time out to study and also defied library etiquette (lock me up and throw away the key!). As I was waddling through each of the aisles, lazily touching books while performing the role of therapist to my friend, I happened to stop in the psychology section. The phone call was distracting me from what I'd planned to do, and now I was distracted from the call — a total mess! A brightly coloured paperback caught my attention, so I picked it up and started flipping through the pages. The cover said, *Personality Plus: How to Understand Others by Understanding Yourself* by Florence Littauer. I remember not being able to comprehend how learning about someone else could tell me about myself, but at that point all I was reading was erotic fiction, so I felt like I had the intellectual space to consume this new concept.

As I flicked through *Personality Plus* on the commute home, I was surprised to come across terms I hadn't seen before. As a self-proclaimed personality-test connoisseur, I thought I'd seen it all. Not quite! The book asked me to consider 'what makes *me* so special?'; whether or not I was 'melancholy, choleric, sanguine, or phlegmatic' (what does this all mean?!); and what my archetype was (huh?). If not for the 30-minute train ride and the shitty reception I would've definitely stopped reading; not because the book was bad, but because I have a short attention span and my muscle memory makes me use my phone even when I don't mean to.

Littauer explained, 'When we know who we are and why we act the way we do, we can begin to understand our inner selves, improve our personalities and learn to get along with others.' I was sceptical, but very intrigued. The first chapter alone was full of clichés (not a bad thing as they made the ideas more accessible to me), but for some reason, I felt like the book was directed to me. When I picked up *Personality Plus*, I just so happened to be in the middle of a character evolution, and this book made me feel seen. Littauer went on to explain that there is no one like you, so it's naive to assume that there is one universal path to self-betterment. **Because no two people are alike, we shouldn't expect a magic formula that will transform us into the perfect version of ourselves.** As Littauer said, 'Until we recognise our uniqueness, we can't understand how people can sit in the same seminar, with the same people, for the same amount of time and all achieve different degrees of success.'

My! Mind! Was! Blown! Who would've thought the reason why I didn't have what others did or achieved things at the pace they had — regardless of our similar experiences and knowledge — was because I'm a different person! I think this is what one would call an 'epiphany'. I'm explaining this to you so you understand that when it comes to goal setting, knowing what you want is vital; but who you are can determine how you achieve your goals. Knowing that who I am has such an impact on what I do and how I do it made me realise that understanding myself was one of the most important skills I could learn.

Picture this: knowing what you want is like having the ingredients for an amazing recipe. In theory, the meal should've been delicious, but when you attempted to make it, it turned out trash. Why? Some could argue that you didn't have the skill, which is fair; cooking is hard. You saw the journey to creating that meal as binary: I want a five-star meal, I'm going to make it. In reality you didn't acknowledge that to cook well you needed to learn the correct techniques, buy the right utensils and produce, then develop your ability. Only recognising your own abilities and limitations through a practised amount of self-awareness and attention to detail could have prepared you for that. That's why knowing who you are is critical. Not just so you can avoid disaster, and not so you can get exactly what you want, but so your wins aren't just flukes or happy mistakes — they're achievements that you have worked for. You want to get to a place where you know yourself so well that achieving is a no-brainer. Don't get in your own way, the world will do that for you. If you haven't learned how not to be your own barrier, this chapter is where you'll begin to better understand yourself and others. People are unique; we know this. Yes, we may share similar characteristics, but the combinations of those characteristics are what's special. So, naturally, **the way you tackle your objectives should be as unique as you are**. It's dangerous to interpret goals and goal-setting as a one-dimensional practice: 'I'm a person and I want this Thing. Somebody's had the Thing before me, therefore it is possible for me to achieve it.' This way of thinking doesn't take into consideration the fact that people are fundamentally different; we don't all have access to the same resources, skills, abilities, motivations or characteristics.

Acknowledge and accept that you are a complex person.

You are confusing and hard to read, so it will take a little while to consciously learn about yourself. Don't delude yourself into thinking you possess qualities that you don't; that you are patient when you're not, that you have good time-management skills when you know that's not true; that you are able to be objective when that is a big lie.

KNOWING WHO YOU ARE AND HOW YOU REACT TO THINGS WILL HELP YOU MANAGE AND DEAL WITH OBSTACLES.

TASK
WHO ARE YOU?

'You', as a concept, is the amalgamation of how you see yourself, how you want to be seen, how strangers see you, how your loved ones see you, the blind spots you have to your own behaviour and then a void you'll never uncover (I promise we'll come back to this later!).

Before I redirect you to personality tests, I want you to try to evaluate how you interpret yourself without the influence of the outside world. This book will have a number of activities to help you put theory into practice, and I want you to read every chapter feeling like you have the confidence to explore what you've learned.

I want you to have a deep, considered think about the following questions. Answer one in full before you move to the next. There's no rush!

1. What are three things you like about yourself?

2. What are three things you dislike about yourself?

3. What do people misunderstand about you?

4. What are your fears?

5. What are you grateful for?

6. What would you change about yourself?

7. What would you never change about yourself?

8. What can make you difficult to be around?

9. If you had three rules for life, what would they be?

10. What are your three most important values?

11. What do you think your family, your best friends and your boss would say your strengths and weaknesses are?

Now let's reflect on how you evaluated yourself:

Was the task easy or hard for you, and why?

Have you ever thought about yourself to that degree before? If not, why? If yes, how often? What's encouraged you to think about yourself that way in the past?

How different is the way you are perceived by the outside world versus how you see yourself? Why do you think this is?

Now, you are officially a few degrees closer to knowing who you actually are. The point of this exercise isn't to stress you out or propel you to immediate change. This exercise is devised to give you a clearer idea of your starting point. Think of your personality and character traits as different tools in your toolbox, all of which can be used when required. Personally, I can be very opinionated, bold and charming, so I search for opportunities that allow me to use those skills, like public speaking. I can speak at length comfortably when given a topic I know. Podcasting, TV presenting and hosting are all career paths that allow me to utilise those skills, and when I'm in these spaces I feel secure.

Practising self-awareness is a reminder to stay in touch with yourself: to know who you think you are, and how others perceive you.

If you're not focused on how you come across, you can find yourself having trouble understanding why you're not being interpreted in a way that resonates. People often mistake my confidence and charisma for a lack of insecurity. They assume that because I put myself out there that I don't have boundaries around how far out of my comfort zone I'm willing to go. In the past, that has resulted in me having to unjustly prove why I don't want to do certain jobs, try new foods, go to new places or try experiences that from the outside may seem like they're perfect for my personality.

I was once offered a gig hosting a corporate event for a pharmaceutical brand. The job would have required me to learn pages and pages of script full of medical jargon, which had been approved by ten (this is an exaggeration) CEOs and other important people, meaning I'd have no freedom to improvise. There was so much red tape! They wanted me for my 'vivacious and energetic presence' and they 'loved the way I spoke so comfortably'. I appreciated the compliment, but what they didn't understand — and what I found hard to communicate to them — was my level of experience was based on my comfort levels. I'm a TV presenter, so people assume that I can read, memorise and regurgitate information, when in reality most of what I do is off the cuff and unscripted (like sitting in my house ranting about pop culture, chatting about chicken salt and menstrual cups); these are obviously two very different skills. I'm naturally good at the latter and really struggle with the former. **I prioritise jobs that fit within the confines of my skillset, and recognise that I'm in a position in my career where I'm privileged enough to put my comfort first.**

I declined the opportunity from the pharmaceutical brand, explaining as best I could that I didn't feel equipped with the skills to recite a heavily scripted monologue (of things I didn't understand or really care to) and perhaps they should find someone better suited to the industry and role. This response was met with confusion: 'What do you mean? You'd be perfect! You do this all the time!' Which, again, was fair and very flattering. But all this response did was make me ponder, *'Am I who I think I am, or who others think I am?'* If more people recognise a version of me that's more capable than I give myself credit for, wouldn't it be beneficial to lean into that perception? Maybe so, but I have spent enough time in unfamiliar situations that lie on a spectrum from 'awkward, but bearable' to 'will haunt and scar me for life due to a negative outcome' that I now know where I draw the line (turns out, it's somewhere in the middle). Sometimes I'll take a dip on either side of the spectrum to remind myself that I have choices. Of course, there are some instances in which you'd fight through discomfort for the greater good (say, if Michelle and Barack Obama wanted to me to MC their twentieth wedding-anniversary party), but this didn't feel like one of those situations. Based on what I understood of myself, what the pharmaceutical company was asking just didn't feel like 'me', and that was the hill I would comfortably die on.

SELF-
AWARENESS

Definition: *The act of examining yourself through a critical, objective lens. To understand who you are and why. To notice what you're doing and why. To notice how you feel and why. To acknowledge what you want and why.*

Once you see that self-awareness isn't just knowing that you're doing stuff, but understanding why you are the way you are, you may suddenly realise that sometimes we just don't know why we do ANYTHING. Why do I aspire for money and career recognition? Why is it important to me to express my creativity? Why don't I drink eight glasses of water a day? Why do I believe I have agency? Why don't I opt out of capitalism and live off the grid with pet chihuahuas?

It's so easy (and predictable) to talk about the experiences that might have pushed us towards certain behaviours or prevented us from reaching particular milestones, but that's almost redundant if we don't unpack the *WHY*. Not the Why that's easiest to theorise. Not the Why that's the quickest story to tell. Not the Why that makes you sound smart. The *actual* Why. That's the challenging bit, and I'm not judging you if you don't know what that is just yet. It's hard!

I keep noticing that people would rather fake self-awareness than say that they honestly have no idea why they do what they do. Admitting this feels like a very important step; what's the benefit of pretending? Why have we stigmatised introspection so much? Probably because we've all been indoctrinated into the 'fake it till you make it' school of thought — the one that tells you to explicitly disregard reality in favour of an imagined existence (which is definitely beneficial as part of a bigger picture involving making it and then behaving honestly). But the phrase is fake it until you make it, not fake it forever and ever and ever.

When we're rushing the process of digging deep, we often settle, then allow ourselves to draw easy conclusions. That could be due to a problem-solving theory called Occam's razor, which states that the simplest answer is often correct. But in the case of self-discovery, we're not really after a singular reason, but multiple. When we're building self-awareness, I believe it's less about finding conclusive answers and more about thinking critically and uncovering the ways you're multifaceted. The more options the better, like in the following scenario.

Why do I have such a deep interest in success, money and career?

Because I grew up in a working class, single-parent home where — although I was spoiled, within reason — money (or lack thereof) was always a topic of discussion.

Because the society I've been raised in and the media I engage with encourage me to aspire to achieve, and achievement in this century looks like a lot of things (athleticism, academia, a musical inclination) but the common denominator for all of those is wealth. You know you're killing it when the Thing you're doing well has also made you relatively heaps of money.

Because success, money and career are the areas of my life in which I've been most validated.

Because I haven't seen positive or relatable examples of what life would be like if I didn't aspire for success, money and a 'good' career.

Because all the people I admire have at least one of these things.

Because from a young age, I've been reminded that achieving these things is 'important'. People are always asking, 'What do you want to be when you grow up?', but what they're really asking is 'What career do you aspire to, and how much money will you make?'

Of course, I could stop at one reason and assume that's the truth, the whole truth and the extent of my situation, but with these six options I have a better understanding of myself, and a clearer idea of what influences and drives me. All these answers tell me a lot more about who I am and why.

In my experience, the quickest and most effective way to uncover my motivations and see myself clearly has been through personality typing and basic psychological profiles. No matter how unique people are, we all fall into universal character and personality archetypes regardless of our gender, sexuality, socioeconomic status, demographic, or any other external factors which can influence us. These archetypes impact how we see and express ourselves and how we perceive others.

Don't roll your eyes or skip this page, I'm serious! You wanted the inside scoop, so I'm giving it to you. **Personality tests are not perfect; there are heaps of flaws with the way they work, but your results will accurately reflect the answers you've put in, acting as a mirror of sorts.** The thing is, personality typing requires you to report on yourself (and we've already spoken about how important self-awareness is!) and asks you to look within and accurately assess who you are. This process can be highly subjective because of our personal bias. We might see ourselves as smarter, kinder or more objective than we are, which then affects the final response the test will give us. This process is called response distortion. Some people do it consciously, especially in environments where they know that certain test results could impact them negatively (like at work or in a psychological assessment), and for some it's merely a subconscious action. In other instances, people will see a question, for example, 'Do you talk a lot at parties?' and recall a specific party, rather than thinking about all the parties they've attended and creating an average response based on those collective experiences. Not being able to think more widely about your experiences can also skew your results. For this reason, it's so important not to give aspirational answers when you take a personality test. What I mean by this is that your answer shouldn't be how you *hope* you'd act in a certain situation or how you've acted on one occasion — your answer needs to be a reflection of what you actually do a majority of the time.

It's not that the tests themselves are flawed, but that the people doing the tests are aware of how their own flaws are perceived and because of that they might try to rig the results. It's crucial to understand that these tests aren't going to magically tell you who you are, they're just mirroring the information you've provided and giving you a concise conclusion based on that evidence. It goes without saying that if you don't tell the truth, the results won't either.

With all that in mind, try to be open to doing a test. Best-case scenario, your result will reflect exactly the way you perceive yourself to be and you'll realise that you somersaulted out of the womb as a completely self-aware human. Or neutral-case scenario, you'll finally have a clear way to articulate who you are in ways you might not have previously. Or worst-case scenario — which is still a great result — you find out you have a ton of behavioural, personality and character blind spots you've never considered, and now you have some work to do. Once you know your blind spots, you should tell people. Let the world see you for you really are so they can be aware, praise you or hold you accountable.

Deluding yourself can be helpful in moderation, but an excess dose may have adverse effects.

For the last two years, I've often taken to my Instagram story to ask my audience moral questions: the type of questions that beg for increased self-awareness like, 'Do you think you are, or can be seen as, problematic?' or 'Do you hurt others more than others hurt you?'. These questions then became the basis of my critical thinking card-game ReFlex. The responses to these questions usually feature the same theme. People lean towards the answers they think are more socially acceptable. They'll generally deny the possibility that they're problematic, while swearing that they get hurt more than they hurt others. I'm not saying that people don't have the range to be good, but when I take a look at the world around me, I see that our behaviours fit into the problematic and hurtful categories more than we think.

==It's easy to look at yourself and your intentions through an aspirational or virtuous lens. It's also easier to disregard the impact of your behaviour if you think you had the right intentions.==

Maybe you always carry an enviro-bag to reduce your plastic consumption, yet you still buy produce from huge grocery chains for convenience, disregarding the fact that these companies have adverse impacts on the environment by mass producing. You might be a huge advocate for reducing the impacts of climate change, but you still buy fast fashion because style is important to you, and you don't have enough money to shop more sustainably. Maybe you, personally, aren't bigoted, but you know some of your family and close friends are, and you don't want to confront them because it's awkward. Maybe you support the #MeToo movement, but love dancing to music from alleged abusers because you can make the distinction between supporting the art but not the artist. Maybe you lied about being under twenty-one so you wouldn't have to stop and talk to a volunteer from Greenpeace (it happens).

The examples above aren't rare or unusual, and they're not made to make you feel bad or minimise the good things you've done in your life. However, I reference these scenarios often when I have critical discussions about the nature of being problematic and harmful. When we think of these behaviours, we tend to visualise extreme physical, mental or emotional abuse, often ignoring other potent-yet-passive forms of harm like lying, stealing, capitalising, exploiting, gaslighting, minimising, one-upping, belittling, cheating, or any other more insidious forms of manipulation or harm.

The point is, it's easy not to consider all the layers of your character (especially the ones we'd rather pretend don't exist), particularly when you're under the pressure of being tested; knowing that your results will impact how you feel about yourself. Try not to prioritise quick results over the time it takes you to think about yourself holistically. Stepping away from your mental comforts in order to see yourself through a critical lens is a crucial aspect of self-awareness.

THE JOHARI WINDOW

Self-awareness isn't a destination, but a series of quests that keeps you searching and growing until the end of time. The prize is learning about yourself and improving how you see others.

One fateful night, my best friend Grace asked me in a WhatsApp message if I'd heard of the Johari window. I said no and quickly rushed to Google. Little did I know that my life was about to change. The Johari window is a psychological model that was developed in 1955 by two American psychologists, Joseph Luft and Harry Ingham. In addition to making you more aware you of what you already know about yourself, the Johari window also introduces you to the idea that there are things you don't know and things that you will never know about yourself. It also suggests that you can build the trust of others by revealing information about yourself, and in return you can learn more about who you are through feedback.

A Johari window is made using four quadrants, two of which represent what you know about yourself, while the other two represent the parts unknown to you but known to others. The test requires a subject, which in this case is you. You're given a list of fifty-six adjectives, from which you can pick five to ten that you feel best describe your personality. The list is then given to a few people you think know you well. From there, you ask your chosen people to pick adjectives from the list that they think best describe you. It's important that each party does this without the help of anyone else.

It might also be helpful for them not to pick adjectives in front of you, as that could encourage them to answer differently. Once that's done, compare all the lists and map them in the Johari window.

The idea is that you'll be exposed to how self-aware you are by comparing your subjective self-assessment to other people's evaluations of you. If there were an overwhelming amount of adjectives that popped up that you don't resonate with, it doesn't mean you're not being yourself, but it might mean that you do a poor job of expressing yourself accurately to others. As you learn to self-evaluate, increase your vulnerability and show people who you are, you should ideally get to a point where people see you as you see yourself and vice versa.

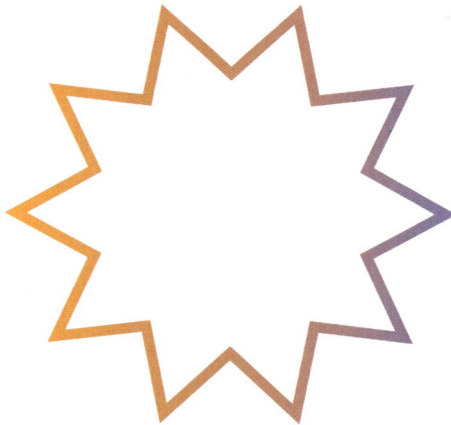

	WHAT YOU SEE IN ME	WHAT YOU DO NOT SEE IN ME
WHAT I SEE IN ME	The Public Self	The Private (or hidden) Self
WHAT I DO NOT SEE IN ME	The Blind Self	The Undiscovered Self

Here's the list of adjectives:

1. ABLE
2. ACCEPTING
3. ADAPTABLE
4. BOLD
5. BRAVE
6. CALM
7. CARING
8. CHEERFUL
9. CLEVER
10. COMPLEX
11. CONFIDENT
12. DEPENDABLE
13. DIGNIFIED
14. EMPATHETIC
15. ENERGETIC
16. EXTROVERTED
17. FRIENDLY
18. GIVING
19. HAPPY
20. HELPFUL
21. IDEALISTIC
22. INDEPENDENT
23. INGENIOUS
24. INTELLIGENT
25. INTROVERTED
26. KIND
27. KNOWLEDGEABLE
28. LOGICAL
29. LOVING
30. MATURE

31. MODEST	46. SENSIBLE
32. NERVOUS	47. SENTIMENTAL
33. OBSERVANT	48. SHY
34. ORGANISED	49. SILLY
35. PATIENT	50. SPONTANEOUS
36. POWERFUL	51. SYMPATHETIC
37. PROUD	52. TENSE
38. QUIET	53. TRUSTWORTHY
39. REFLECTIVE	54. WARM
40. RELAXED	55. WISE
41. RELIGIOUS	56. WITTY
42. RESPONSIVE	
43. SEARCHING	
44. SELF-CENTRED	
45. SELF-CONSCIOUS	

The Johari window test works by adding information to each of the four quadrants. The size of the quadrant windows will shift according to how much information you put in each. For example, if you and the majority of the people who assessed you think you're witty, that trait would be placed in the Public Self quadrant. If you said you were tense but nobody else assessed you that way, then that would be part of your Private Self.

The more open and forthcoming you are, the easier it is for others to identify with you, a trait which will increase the size of your Public Self quadrant. Alternatively, if you are a mysterious or highly secretive person who struggles to connect with others, your Private Self quadrant will be wider.

THE PUBLIC SELF

This is the part of ourselves that we are happy to share with others. Knowledge of the Public Self shows a level of self-awareness, while also meaning you've done a considerable amount of work communicating who you are to the people around you to ensure that they see you in the same way you see yourself. This is why it's important to do this activity with people who know you well, as you've had more time to communicate your true self to them, which means they will have a deeper insight into who you are than a group of acquaintances might. When you meet someone new it's understandable for your Public Self quadrant to be smaller because you haven't had time to exchange information. When you get to chitchatting, this area should expand.

THE PRIVATE SELF

This is the part of yourself that is obvious to you but is too private to share with others. You might be concealing this part of yourself because you're uncomfortable with sharing it with others, embarrassed, ashamed, or perhaps you believe that it wouldn't be well received. You may also avoid sharing these parts of yourself because there needs to be an element of mutual trust before you're prepared to be vulnerable, and for some this is a process which takes longer than others. Trust can be hard to build.

If your Private Self quadrant is especially large, you might frequently feel misinterpreted. **It's easy to see why someone can't comprehend your thoughts and actions if they don't actually know you.**

THE BLIND SELF

People are multidimensional and complex, yet we are often made to feel like we're binary. Sometimes we're public, sometimes private, but how do we account for the in-between?

Have you ever considered that there are some behaviours which others can see clearly in you, but you don't see in yourself? Or, better yet, have you ever noticed behaviours in others that they don't see in themselves? The self-described empathetic friend who's always bitching about her colleagues and is terribly rude to waitstaff. Or the passive-aggressive guy who swears he's an amazing and transparent communicator. It doesn't add up, but that's OK because self-awareness — in this case, the ability to recognise that you'll never truly be able see all of yourself — exists on a spectrum.

Now you might be thinking, *Wait, can't someone just pull me up on my blind spots and help me improve my self-awareness?* In theory, yes, but the whole point of being self-aware is to not rely on others to show you who you are. You may start to prioritise behaving in the way you're perceived instead of how you actually are. In reality, when someone tells you something about yourself that you don't identify with it's unlikely that you'll take that feedback on board. If you're someone who is increasingly open to feedback and improving, you may be more inclined to take this constructive criticism on; however, our personalities and characters have had decades to develop, and we behave in certain ways because it's what's familiar to us.

Even if you've been made aware of a blind spot, it can be difficult to prioritise changing it. Yes, in theory you can overcome your blind spots if you consciously try to unpack and change hidden elements of yourself, but this could take years to unlearn. Alternatively, your Blind Self might reign supreme because you simply aren't as open to change as some. Perhaps it's hard to accept that there are things about yourself that you're blind to, let alone that there could be flaws which might need to be changed.

THE UNDISCOVERED SELF

The Undiscovered Self is undoubtedly the hardest to comprehend, but there are parts of yourself that neither you nor anyone else can see. In simple terms, **you don't know what you've never been able to see, comprehend or encounter.** These behaviours can be good or bad, but it's a little counterintuitive to focus on it until they present themselves and become a part of your Private, Blind or, in the best-case scenario, Public Self. In theory, once the quadrants are populated by you and your chosen people, all the adjectives that don't show up on any assessment of you technically belong in the unknown area.

Character-affirming situations resulting in introspection, or even traumatic scenarios, have the potential to help unlock your Undiscovered Self, but again, it's ideal to focus more on what is known and what needs to be developed, rather than what might never be known.

Out yourself flaws and all.

HOW TO UNLOCK YOUR JOHARI WINDOW

Step one: Find a person who knows you well and ask them to analyse you. Offer to analyse them as well.

Step two: Earlier I suggested you use a notebook to jot down any answers to activities (or general tidbits you learn), so you can reference them easily. Grab this and copy or trace this template of the Johari window:

Name the top left The Public Self (Known to all), the bottom left The Blind Self (Unknown to you), the top right The Private Self (Known to you) and the bottom right The Unknown Self (Unknown to all).

Make an individual table for every person assessing you; I'd recommend keeping them in your notebook as well.

Step three: Using the Johari adjectives list, pick the words you feel best describe your personality, and ask the person (or people) you're participating with to do the same.

Step four: Once both lists are complete, create a new rectangle with four blank quadrants. The top-left quadrant is for words that miraculously landed in both lists — yay! This is your Public Self, and these qualities are what we see in ourselves and happily let others see as well.

Step five: The words you chose but the person analysing you didn't will go in the bottom-left corner. This is your Private Self.

Step six: The words your analyser chose but you didn't are your blind spots, aka your Blind Self. Pop these into the top right-hand corner.

Step seven: Finally, the words not chosen by anyone go in the bottom right. These traits might not resonate with you now, but they could in the future. This is your Undiscovered Self, and can be considered as a potential area for self-evaluation.

Completing a Johari window will likely be a confronting, and at times overwhelming, experience. It's not unusual to feel misunderstood or labelled unfairly. We're rarely in environments that encourage this level of introspection, so don't feel boxed in (pun intended) by the results. After all, it's just information, and this is only one of at least 100,000 ways to get to know yourself.

HOW TO FURTHER ANALYSE YOUR JOHARI WINDOW RESULTS

The information you have now is more than enough to illuminate the depths of your character. If you're anything like me and are feverish at the thought of further self-analysis, read on to satisfy that craving! There are four distinct personas to look out for, and you'll find yours by identifying which quadrant has the most words.

Open Persona

This means that the majority of your adjectives landed in the Public-Self quadrant. The presumption is that people with an open persona are able to show themselsves and others their truest self with minimal effort. They're also really aware of how they come across to others.

People with an open persona can be seen as easy-going and relaxed. They are more likely to know who they are and have come to terms with themselves — or at least have a lot less shame about being who they are than others might. Open personas are rarely preoccupied or anxious when socialising, mostly likely because they are well-adjusted.

However, it's worth making the distinction between the two sides of the open-persona spectrum. The first side is someone who's open because they're vulnerable and easily able to present who they are versus someone who overshares because they have a desire to connect, often prematurely. While the former will be more adjusted, the latter may overshare due to feelings of inadequacy and potential narcissistic tendencies, which lead them to speak a lot as a means to reroute the conversation to themself. The reasons may vary, but I digress. The Johari window method should only be used as a reference point for self-exploration, not to armchair-diagnose.

Naive Persona

This result means you have the most words in the Blind Self window, and very little in Public Self or Private Self. Naive personas are yet to discover the many facets of their personalities. These personas are not avoidant about who they are, rather they have a general ignorance about themselves. People who score high in the Blind Self area could also be perceived as being a little oblivious or delusional.

You can either be seen as a naive person who is so unaware of themselves that it's endearing, or people may think that you're annoyingly untouchable, refusing to let anyone or any feedback in. Maybe it's somewhere in between.

The glaring concern for naive personas is that if you don't have the range to see yourself, how can you dig deep to find the right areas to improve? Also, how will you have the capacity to truly see others? Discovering that you're a naive persona is a really awesome opportunity to increase your Public Self by asking for feedback from your peers, and then doing some good old soul-searching.

Secret Persona

This means you have the most words in Private Self and the least in Public Self. Perhaps you're happy to let people call you mysterious, or maybe you're just secretive and closed-off. You might seem really distant and detached to the average person, or maybe people tell you they struggle to connect with you. This persona isn't completely sustainable as you'll likely spend a lot of unnecessary energy trying to hide parts of yourself from others, but each to their own.

WHICH
PERSONALITY
TEST IS RIGHT
FOR YOU?

If you sprinted to Google to type in that question you'd get a hundred vague results, which would ultimately confuse you. To make your life easier, I'm going to list a few of my favourite personality tests, a brief description of what they promise, where to find them, their various pros and cons, and my own results for comparison. I've ordered the tests from beginner-friendly to the most advanced, which provide professional introspection. The tests are simply here to give you insight into yourself. If the results don't resonate with you that's fine, it's not a perfect science.

==Whatever you do, don't start adopting personality traits because an algorithm on the internet said it perceives you a certain way.==

The Barnum effect:

The Barnum effect is a very common bias that happens when someone believes that a personality description they've heard or read about applies specifically to them without considering that the information is generic and could resonate with anyone: 'You're always thinking and you can be moody when you're hungry', then you think 'Wow, this is SO ME!' This is often seen in astrology, psychic readings, hypnosis, mentalists, tarot readings, and yes, even personality typing.

Don't forget that these tests give the results which are closest to the data you input. They feed this information back to you in a way that's easy to digest. While the tests show you the result that matches your personality the most, a computer-generated test doesn't actually know you. Don't be the gullible person who believes that vague, sweeping statements are their core identifiers! Use these results in *addition* to introspection, not *instead* of.

The Barnum effect came from an experiment conducted in 1948 by Professor Bertram R. Forer. He handed his students a personality test and claimed (lol, lied!) that their results would be analysed and the students would be given an individually tailored assessment in return.

Naturally, the joke was on the students. Forer didn't assess the test or give them individual feedback, instead he gave them each a paragraph of generalised statements like:

Sometimes you give too much effort on projects that don't work out.

You are an independent thinker who takes pride in doing things differently than others.

You worry about your future but are hopeful that things will work out well.

It gets even more laughable. Forer then asked the students to evaluate how much their results resonated with them, giving each result a rating between zero and five — with five being the most accurate, and zero being the least. The average rating was 4.26. I'M YELLING! To this day, this experiment continues and holds an impressive 'accuracy' record.

The reason we get fooled by these vague assertions is because of cognitive bias. This basically means that if we hear something that resonates with us — good or bad — we'll believe it as fact rather than questioning it, as it confirms what we already suspected. So, as you read the results of your personality tests and find yourself living, loving and agreeing with everything, take a second to question whether or not it truly is a representation of you or if it's general enough to apply to anyone.

Disclaimer:

Before we begin the comprehensive review of all the personality tests I've taken, I will stress that for every single one (where possible and if it's available), I recommend you use verified versions which are, more often than not, the paid versions. The most obvious reason is that I don't want to advocate for piracy, and it's safe to assume that free tests have been unlawfully copied and redistributed without giving rights to the owner.

Despite the flaws of personality typing, these examples are made with psychometrics in mind, which is a system used to measure the quality of a test. The two factors of a 'good' test are reliability (using a consistent process to measure responses, so you could take it multiple times and get consistent results), and validity (whether it accurately measures your responses).

The experts say that reliability and validity is what makes a fun-only quiz different to a psychometric assessment. In the latter, you're buying the test from someone respected and vetted, who has a stake in providing you with a high-quality test. If the test is trash or inconsistent, their whole reputation is on the line. Making sure a personality test is legit is an expensive process, which takes time to measure, assess and evaluate, and obviously requires a level of expertise that free quizzes generally don't have.

Look for validated, legitimate versions of tests, which are endorsed by scientists, psychologists and psychiatrists. The money you pay not only supports these professionals and their craft but also provides you with pages and pages and pages of information pertaining to your type. It's worth it.

THE BIG FIVE

WHAT IS IT?

The Big Five test measures your personality based on five major types:

Openness — how open you are to new ideas and experiences

Conscientiousness — how goal-oriented and organised you are

Agreeableness — how likely you are to put other people's needs above your own

Extroversion — how much you're energised by others

Neuroticism — how much you're negatively impacted by stress and other emotional triggers.

HOW DOES IT WORK?

The test asks you to respond to a series of statements about yourself — everything from 'I feel I am better than other people' to 'I get chores done right away' — with a scale ranging from disagree, neutral to agree. In this test, a higher ranking doesn't necessarily equal a good result, it just shows you how the quantity of traits you have can impact your personality and how you work.

For example, in this test, 'extraversion' refers to how much you assert yourself and how social or excitable you are. Scoring high in extraversion can mean that you are charming, outgoing and gain energy when you're in the company of other people. However, a lower score could mean you're more reserved and prefer your own company. In the Big Five, 'agreeableness' refers to how kind, altruistic, or cooperative you are. High scores can mean you're easy-going, empathetic and understanding; while a lower score means you might be seen as hard to work with or less flexible.

Fun fact: In 2019, *The Ascent* published a survey titled, 'Study: Are you too nice to be financially successful?'. They found that your Big Five personalities can intersect with how happy you are in your career, how much money you make, whether you're a spender or saver and if you're likely to pay more for convenience. It's important to note that they only surveyed 509 people, so it's not a huge sample size but it's interesting, nonetheless. Of the people surveyed:

Those who scored really high in extraversion reported being satisfied with their finances, while those who scored high in openness to experiences were the least likely to feel satisfied.

Those who scored high in neuroticism had the highest average salary, while people who scored high in agreeableness had the lowest.

Those who scored high in conscientiousness were more likely to identify as being savers, but extroverts were most likely to say they were spenders (as an extrovert, I feel seen).

Highly scoring extroverts were more likely to file their taxes on time and negotiate a lower price for expensive stuff, like flights and holidays.

WHERE TO FIND IT?

You can take the test online via Truity.com. The Big Five test is estimated to take ten minutes to complete, but I've no doubt you could zoom through it in five.

PROS:

The verified, legitimate version is free (yay!).

The site is easy to use; no bells and whistles.

The questions are really accessible and they've left the big words at the door.

You can do it quickly and online.

THE BIG FIVE

THE BIG FIVE

The results are brief, and as with the questions, they're written in a way that's simple to understand.

The site provides links to supporting information, FAQs and further reading.

CONS:

The results are brief, which means they can be vague.

The questions can feel too simple, and it's not always clear why they've been asked (why are we talking about chores?!).

You'll probably finish the test with more questions than answers.

MY RESULTS:

O	98%
C	46%
E	81%
A	23%
N	29%

0 10 20 30 40 50 60 70 80 90 100

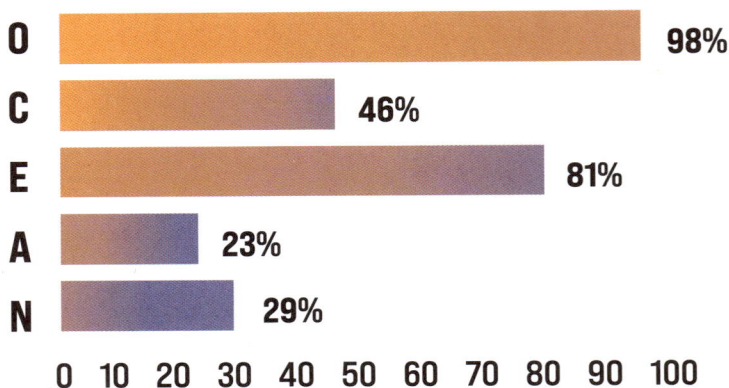

Openness describes a person's tendency to think in abstract and complex ways. I scored crazy-high in this category, which suggests that I am creative, adventurous, intellectual and more likely to seek out complex forms of self-expression. Hello, THAT IS ME TO A TEE! Alternatively, a low score in openness means you prefer to focus on practical pursuits; while I'm an imaginative person, I do also seek out logical ways of doing and viewing things.

The Big Five is one of the few legit online personality tests that is developed by a psychometrics company and is FREE to take (generally you'd be parting with some kind of coin for something of this calibre). Because it costs you a total of zero dollars to participate, the results you get are brief (you get what you pay for), however it is possible to purchase a fuller report for a small fee. Now generally I'd recommend you pay for more insight, but as the Big Five is not my preferred test, I've stuck with my initial results.

It's worth knowing that these free results only tell you what it means if you score high in a specific area, and not how you're perceived if you score high in multiple areas. Without the additional data, the results can feel a bit confusing and contradictory because they don't provide extensive information on these varied sides of your personality. In my results it clarifies that I'm open to experiences and an extrovert, but what do those two results combined mean? The Big Five is a great stepping-stone in the world of personality typing, and I've got heaps of other tests to offer that may tickle your fancy just a little bit more.

THE BIG FIVE

THE FOUR TEMPERAMENTS (DISC)

What is it?

Popularly referred to as the DISC model, this test works on the assumption that most people have predictable patterns of behaviour (lol, tea), which are a blend of four temperament types. These types are Dominance (Choleric), Inspiring/Influence (Sanguine), Supportive/Steadiness (Phlegmatic) and Cautious/Conscientiousness (Melancholic), and they come together to create a four-part circle. The test recognises that every person shows aspects of each of these types within their personality; however, it focuses on the one or two temperaments that best represents you.

HOW DOES IT WORK?

The test looks to find how your behaviour changes in different situations. It aims to reveal how you respond to barriers, rules and challenges, as well as the speed at which you like to work. It doesn't measure every facet of your personality, only those four distinct areas.

Fun fact: The Four Temperaments test stresses that there needs to be a clear distinction between a trait and a type. Types are considered to be categories into which a person will either fit or not. For example, a person could be seen as either an extrovert or introvert. Temperament, on the other hand, represents the way a person relates to others and responds to situations. A temperament is the behaviour which, after observing someone, you'd expect them to display.

The temperaments are represented by four distinct groups of traits or tendencies. Each cluster of traits produces a specific behaviour that is different from the other groups.

PROS:

It's super simple to remember your trait because there are only four to pick from.

The test gives you an easy and comprehensive understanding on how to assess yourself, but also how to assess others and get a better understanding of why they communicate or react the way they do.

You'll receive a personalised report with background information on DISC, customised graphs to show you how you scored, and a seven-step activity to make you a 'better you' and improve the relationships in your life.

CONS:

The test doesn't really assess specific skills or how your trait can be interpreted in different environments or by other people.

Two individuals can share exactly the same DISC scores and yet somehow come across as completely different people. Similar to skills and traits, the test doesn't take into consideration things like emotional IQ (EQ) and individual motivators. For example, a dominant person with a high EQ can be seen as assertive and decisive, yet someone with a low EQ, can come across as aggressive, demanding and confrontational.

MY RESULTS:

I rank highly in both Dominance and Inspiring/Influence; which experts say is a very rare combination. I'm categorised as an assertive person who can be direct and focused when needed, but I can also be charming and prioritise relationships and emotions if the situation calls for it. My results suggest that I'm driven by two main motivators, the need to get results and to be accepted socially. The combination of these two mean that I often seek out environments where I can be the leader, both professional and personally. But unlike people who just rank highly in Dominance, I also need to know that I'm respected and liked by the people dealing with me.

DISC

MYERS–BRIGGS TYPE INDICATOR (MBTI)

WHAT IS IT?

Now we're getting into popular-typing territory. If you've worked in a modern, corporate office, you've probably heard someone ask, 'What's your Myers–Briggs?'. Or maybe you've seen the classic dating-profile with the four-letter MBTI cushioned between emojis and 'adventure, beach, summer'. If none of this makes sense, let me break it down for you.

HOW DOES IT WORK?

Myers–Briggs is a personality test that assesses how you soak in information and interact with the world and people around you. I should preface this by saying that MBTI doesn't like to be referred to as a test, but rather a tool that provides you with personal insight and helps you become a better version of yourself by pointing out what may prevent you from being your best self and areas where you naturally excel. The 'tool' consists of one hundred and thirty questions like, 'Do you prefer the unplanned or the meticulously arranged event?' or 'Do you like buying things or having the option to buy?' The answers to these questions will determine your personality out of sixteen different types.

Once assessed, you're shown four distinct scales:

1. ***Extrovert to Introvert:*** where do you direct your energy?
   a. An extroverted person is referred to as being more outwardly focused. They like to be seen, heard and can easily be described as outgoing people who like being the centre of attention.
   b. An introverted person is referred to as being more inwardly focused. They're more private and reserved, and prefer to think and observe before acting.

2. *Intuition or Sensing:* how do you prefer to take in information?

    a. An intuitive person is the type who loves to imagine all the possibilities of how things could be. They're big picture people who prefer ideas and concepts and are intrigued by how everything connects.

    b. A sensing person prefers to focus on the reality of how things are not how they could be. They're detail-oriented people who prioritise facts and practicality. They're also very literal.

3. *Thinking or Feeling:* how do you prefer to make decisions?

    a. A thinker prefers to make decisions using logic and rational reasoning. They're great debaters as they enjoy finding the flaws in an argument.

    b. A feeler prefers to make decisions based on their personal values and ethics. They're often described as empathetic people who are ruled by their heart and not their head.

4. *Judging or Perceiving:* how do you prefer to govern your life?

    a. A judging person is known to be a meticulous planner and a generally principled person. They prefer rules and deadlines, winners and losers, right and wrong.

    b. A perceiving person is known to go with the flow and let situations evolve based on the mood. They're more likely to see rules and deadlines merely as guidelines.

Based on how you answered the questions, the test will explain where you sit on the spectrum of each scale. Do you lean more towards introversion or extroversion? Maybe you skew towards thinking more than feeling? Once you know exactly where you sit, you adopt the letter of the side you lean closer towards. There are sixteen possible letter combinations, resulting in sixteen different types of personalities.

MBTI

MBTI

The results of the test are detailed and explain your strengths and weaknesses, what makes you different, what makes you tick, how to understand others, how your type is perceived in childhood versus adulthood, how your type behaves in relationships, what angers you, what types you're most compatible with and, best of all, what the heck to do with all this information.

Fun fact: Between the ages of eighteen and twenty-four, I was hell-bent on categorising every platonic or romantic friend I had using that MBTI system. This was a double-edged sword in a lot of ways. On one hand, categorising my relationships gave me insight into better ways of dealing with people, as it clearly showed me what they excelled at and what they struggled with. The test also explained why I'd had trouble interpreting the way others viewed their experiences, as I struggled to really understand how they could be any different from my own.

As a young'un, I believed that sharing a gender, age, postcode and interests meant that two people should, in theory, be very similar. At one point, I thought that any other teenage girl who lived in the Eastern Suburbs of Sydney and liked pop culture must have the same life experience to mine. We both liked Beyoncé and wore clothes from Supré, what else was there?

Naturally, when you grow up a little and notice that your interests deviate from your friends', you might start to think you're growing apart, your incompatibility meaning you can no longer be friends. The hindsight of adulthood shows us that's not true, but adolescence is a confusing time. **Discovering personality tests gave a lot of my friendships a second chance, just when I thought we were pivoting in different directions. The tests gave me the patience to see that everyone is impacted differently by the world around them and that affects how they behave**. I began to understand why some people were predisposed to people-pleasing, why others prioritised how they felt over logic and why some of us were more comfortable with change than others.

However, at one point I took this testing a bit too far. The tests convinced me (or maybe I'd convinced myself) that everyone had to fit into one of sixteen neat little categories. I started to believe that if people didn't identify with their test results, they just weren't self-aware enough to answer the questions properly. Or, when people didn't act exactly as their result suggested they would, I'd flip out and presume that they were withholding their 'real' selves and were trying to get one up on me. Ha! The nerve of teenage Lil … I think I also used my understanding of the MBTI as a power trip. It gave me an overwhelming sense of confidence, which made me feel like I knew people better than they knew themselves, just because I'd studied each type to death. At times it began to feel like I'd prioritise categorising people over connecting with them. Fear not, I've since checked my neurosis and dealt with that. I can now accept that people are allowed to deviate from their own standards.

PROGS:

The questions are not complicated or elaborately worded.

The test and its results are great tools for personal development and building self-awareness.

There are no 'bad' or undesirable types because none are considered inherently negative, all personality traits are seen as valuable parts of the human experience.

It's popular and widely used, which means the results consider different people in varied circumstances.

It gives you context for how people with your type behave as children, parents and in a romantic relationship.

It helps you identify blind spots in behaviour by explaining clearly how your type can be perceived by others.

MBTI

MBTI

Your results show you what other types you naturally get along with.

You also get an interactive learning session, which will guide you through how the MBTI system actually works and how they got your results.

You'll receive a downloadable report with an overview of your type and links to additional resources.

Many of the MBTI types are matched with the careers best suited to them.

CONS:

Beware the MBTI Kool-Aid: one-part delusion, one-part overconfidence and two-parts homogeny pusher. What I mean by this is that the MBTI can give you false ideas about people — you want to try to avoid thinking that everyone fits neatly into one category. As I learned the hard way, the test makes it easy to believe that you 'get' people just because you know their type. Be conscious of becoming dependent on over-generalised, stereotypical perceptions of types.

The extreme spectrums of results (introverted versus extroverted, intuitive versus sensitive) make you feel like you're stuck on one end of the scale, unable to relate to people on the opposite side.

Although no type is inherently bad, MBTI is one of the few tests that lists out all your negative qualities. There might be a tendency to use your type as an excuse not to improve; 'Of course I suck at remembering little details, I'm an ENTP.'

Critics of MBTI frequently point out that the method is way too simple to accurately measure personality and is therefore unreliable. Studies have shown that when people take the test for the second time, up to fifty per cent get different results.

MY RESULTS:

I'm an ENTP, which is referred to as the Enterprising Explorer and The Assertive Debater. At our best, ENTPs are creative, challenging, curious, theoretical, outspoken, rational, independent and resourceful people who enjoy complex challenges and winning. We're often known to play devil's advocate, because mental sparring is fun, and it helps us to get a sense of other people's reasonings and values. We aggressively bulldoze through new ideas, because there's no better way to raise that good ol' IQ than to attack, poke, prod and question from every angle. We can be annoying and very tiring to be around, I know.

MBTI

ENNEAGRAM

WHAT IS IT?

I don't want to be dramatic, but I've saved the best for last. I love this test like it's my firstborn, like the last hot chip in the bottom of the Maccas bag when you thought you'd run out or that feeling when someone cancels on you when you'd been meaning to flake on them. Simply euphoric.

The Enneagram is a system of nine personality types. Assessment tools are available to help in identifying your personality type. My favorite is offered by The Enneagram Institute and is known as the Riso-Hudson Enneagram Type Indicator, or 'RHETI'. With the RHETI, you answer a set of questions to reveal which of the nine personality types is dominant for you. Sometimes there are two or three personality types that may score highly on the test and then you can learn more about each type to narrow down which one is the most dominant for you. Each of the types are interconnected based on where they sit on the circle. It sounds complicated, and it is a little, but bear with me.

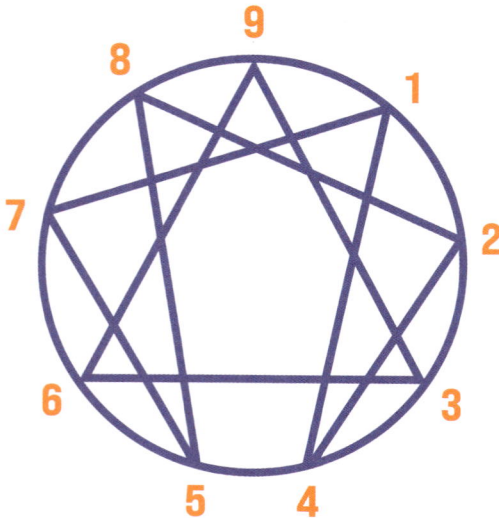

How does it work?

The Enneagram is a complicated test that focuses on how all of the nine main personality types intersect and overlap with each other. It's not as straightforward as the other tests and can at times be difficult to understand; consider this your fair warning. With a whopping 144 statements that will take you an estimated forty minutes to answer, this personality test asks you the most and takes the longest to complete out of all of the options I've suggested. Throughout the assessment you're given pairs of statements and must choose one that describes your general behaviour. The instructions stress that you should choose answers based on your actual reactions, not your aspirational ones. The test also warns that, in some instances, you may identify with both answers but you just have to pick which is true more often. When taking the test, it's best not to overanalyse the questions because your results will be more accurate if you answer spontaneously.

Experts believe that we are all born with one dominant type, which determines how we behave and see the world. The Enneagram's nine types are broken down into centres or triads, which are three groups with three types in each. These numbers interact with those directly next to them chronologically, and this is called the 'Wing'. If you're getting confused, it's OK, I'll go into more detail, just keep reading.

Once you finish the test and your results have been calculated, you'll be sent a detailed document that lists the types and what you scored for each. You'll be given information on the three types you ranked the highest in, which tells you how you're generally perceived, what you desire from life, your hidden side, which of your traits can cause conflict, potential relationship issues you may experience, tips for personal growth and examples of renowned people who share your type. The results will also give you the lowdown on how you act when you're in a standard state of mind, compared to when you're healthy, unhealthy, secure, stressed or growing. It's a lot to take in, but it's worth it.

ENNEAGRAM

ENNEAGRAM

Here's a brief overview of all nine types and their needs, desires and fears.

Type One (*The need to be perfect*):

Type Ones are described as moral perfectionists who desire goodness and integrity, while fearing corruptness or being perceived as 'bad'. This type can struggle with hypocrisy, and they hold a lot of resentment for those who they consider to be immoral or unethical. When in a stressed state, they can be perceived as a Type Four, but while growing they're seen as a Type Seven.

Type Two (*The need to be needed*):

Type Twos are seen as supportive advisors who crave love but fear losing it. They can struggle with denying their own needs and feeling manipulated or manipulating others as a defence mechanism. When stressed they are perceived as an Eight, and in growth a Four.

Type Three (*The need to succeed*):

These are the successful achievers who yearn to feel valued and fear being worthless. They can struggle with vanity and often push themselves to extremes, trying to always be seen as the best. When stressed they are perceived as a Nine, and in growth a Six.

Type Four (*The need to be special or unique*):

Generally thought of as romantic individualists who want to be regarded as uniquely themselves, this type are deathly afraid of having no identity or feeling insignificant. They can struggle with being overly emotional and melancholic, in addition to constantly over-analysing in an attempt to figure out who they are. When stressed they are perceived as a Two, and in growth a One.

Type Five (*The need to understand*):

Type Fives are investigative thinkers who want to understand everything: concepts, theories, idea, life and love. They fear incompetence (both in themselves and others) and feeling like they are incapable. They prefer to live in their head and struggle with doing, often forgoing life experiences in favour of understanding the concept. When stressed they are perceived as a Seven, and in growth an Eight.

Type Six (*The need to be certain*):

This type are loyal guardians who crave support and guidance. They're plagued with indecision, doubt and often seek reassurance. Sixes can struggle with cowardice, stepping up to take opportunities and believing in themselves. When stressed they are perceived as a One, and in growth a Nine.

Type Seven (*The need to avoid pain*):

These are the entertaining optimists who want to feel satisfied and content, but struggle with FOMO. They often think that fulfillment is somewhere else, at the next event, the next movie, the next idea — and this makes it hard for them to truly appreciate being in the moment. When stressed they are perceived as a One, and in growth a Five.

Type Eight (*The need to protect*):

Type Eight are protective challengers who want to feel safe, protected and free from discomfort. They fear being controlled, put in danger or taken advantage of. This type often believe that they are completely self-sufficient people who don't need anything from anyone. This is a defence mechanism, which protects them but also inhibits them from connecting with others easily. When stressed they are perceived as a Five, and in growth a Two.

Type Nine (*The need to be safe*):

The final type are peaceful mediators who crave the nirvana-state feeling of peace of mind. They dread loss or being separated from people and things they love. Type Nines can be conflict avoidant and

ENNEAGRAM

often don't feel like they have the power to assert themselves. When stressed they are perceived as a Six, and in growth a Three.

Similar to any personality test, once you get a good understanding of each type the Enneagram is chock-full of personality stereotypes: Threes are self-absorbed overachievers who are obsessed with how they're perceived; Twos are sweet as pie, ready to lend a hand to literally anyone who needs it, but because of this they can become martyrs; Ones are particular, principled and matter-of-fact, but they can be judgemental because literally no one else see the world in the rigid way they do. But there's more to the Enneagram than just understanding the basic types — I did warn you it was going to get complicated!

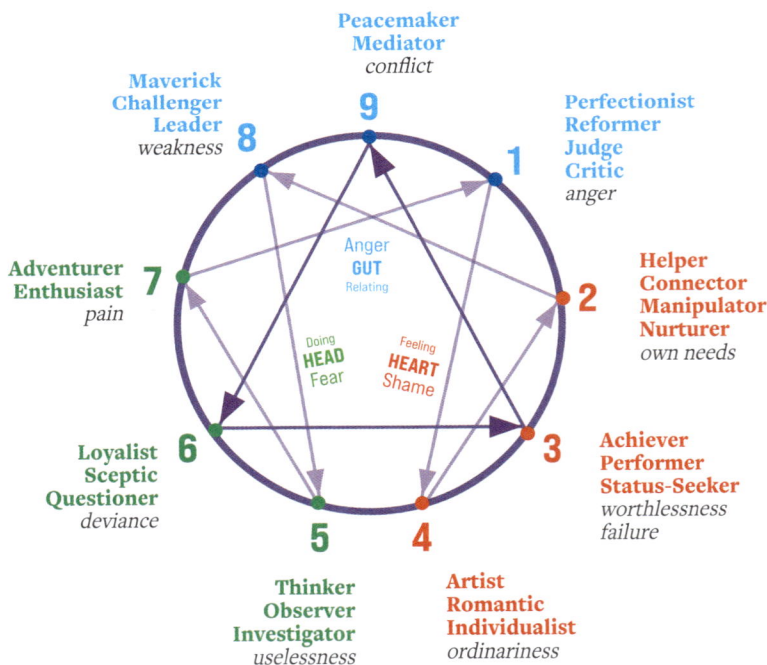

Peacemaker
Mediator
conflict

Maverick
Challenger
Leader
weakness

Perfectionist
Reformer
Judge
Critic
anger

Anger
GUT
Relating

Adventurer
Enthusiast
pain

Helper
Connector
Manipulator
Nurturer
own needs

Doing
HEAD
Fear

Feeling
HEART
Shame

Loyalist
Sceptic
Questioner
deviance

Achiever
Performer
Status-Seeker
worthlessness
failure

Thinker
Observer
Investigator
uselessness

Artist
Romantic
Individualist
ordinariness

Here's a slightly more complicated Enneagram diagram that details how advanced the system can get.

The bold words are simple characteristics to help you identify each type.

The italicised words detail the basic fear or situations each type would avoid.

The arrows show how each type can act or be perceived when they're stressed or growing.

The nine types are also divided into three separate clusters, these are the triads I mentioned earlier. Triads present the issues we have and reveal things we're unhealthily focused on, which can limit our self-development and actualisation. Our triads are good indicators of what we could do less or more of, as well as shows us some of our blind spots and weaknesses.

Experts say that building relationships with people from different triads could offer some balance, getting the mind, body and soul (or in this case, the head, heart and gut) in order. In addition to being perceived as one way when you're in a standard state, stressed and healthy, your triad also has a list of issues and concerns that affects the whole group.

Hoo-boy, we're not done yet. The wing system of the Enneagram test is the final factor in this method of profiling. As we move from childhood into adulthood, we begin to realise how complex we are. The Enneagram suggests that everyone is a unique mixture of their highest-scoring type and the two types adjacent to it. Your basic type is your main personality and the wing is your secondary or complementary personality. Everyone has two wings, but one is generally dominant and more noticeable.

Like most personality tests, you can be tempted to mirror the results you're given. Instead of dismissing what doesn't resonate with you, we sometimes prefer to mimic a stereotype because it's nice to feel seen and understood. The problem is that humans are often paradoxical,

ENNEAGRAM

ENNEAGRAM

and that means our behaviours can be contradictory. Can't I be both self-absorbed and helpful? Can't I be rigid and adventurous? Unlike other tests, the Enneagram takes all the facets of your personality into detailed consideration.

Fun fact: The Enneagram isn't mentioned much in psychology or psychometrics the way other personality tests are. The popularity of this test is due to how heavily it's referenced in modern forms of Christianity. Some believe it's less about deducing the nine types of people and more about discovering the path back to your true self (as many have 'strayed from God' and into 'worldly pleasures'). Others even believe that the Enneagram helps people understand why they may be drawn to certain flaws, going so far as to attribute a deadly sin to each type.

Type One: Anger

Type Two: Pride

Type Three: Deceit

Type Four: Envy

Type Five: Avarice (Greed)

Type Six: Fear

Type Seven: Gluttony

Type Eight: Lust

Type Nine: Sloth

PROS:

Uses no-bullshit, matter-of-fact and direct language.

This test is not fluffy: it acknowledges that at any time you can be healthy, self-sabotaging or stressed and that these things can all have an effect on your personality.

The document that accompanies your results cites references on where the information was found.

The connecting lines in your results show how each basic type has valuable strengths, while at the same time highlighting your darker sides and fears.

The Enneagram is a great tool for understanding yourself and others; it gives you a comprehensive list of your perceived strengths and weaknesses, as opposed to some tests which only highlight the feel-good traits, something which can be deceiving when trying to build self-awareness.

It offers skills for conflict resolution and emotional development by spilling the tea on how you can evolve.

The test can pinpoint your basic fears and motivations, showing how you're being triggered on your journey to evolution.

Provides insight into your repetitive thought and behaviour patterns, giving advice on how you can overcome the negative ones.

CONS:

It's not the most beginner-friendly test and is best taken if you're already on a path to self-development.

The way the results are structured can be hard to comprehend.

It can be easy to mistype yourself. If you rank highly in more than one type, the Enneagram suggests you choose the number that suits you best.

The results show you how many scores you get for each type, rather than a definitive single answer. This can be vague and often requires a lot of additional research.

The origins of the Enneagram are rooted in the occult and Christianity (Catholicism), which can be off-putting for some.

ENNEAGRAM

ENNEAGRAM

MY RESULTS:

I'm an Enneagram Type Three, Wing Type Four (it's complicated, I know), which is commonly known as the Performer or the Achiever. When we're in a healthy frame of mind, we're success-oriented, preoccupied with how we look, adaptable, obsessed with winning and driven for more. According to the test, our basic fear is being worthless; most people in my type just want to feel valued. We're motivated by positive affirmations, constantly trying to distinguish ourselves from others and proving how unique we are. If there was a prize for most impressive, we'd risk everything to win it.

Threes want to make sure their lives are a success, and the irony of that is not lost on me. We're aware that success is defined by the individual. For some, it can mean having a lot of money, a mansion worthy of MTV Cribs and a lavish car with many drink holders. Some strive for academia and others forward-roll into socially focused pursuits like acting, modelling, writing or posting their thoughts online for money. No matter how success is defined, Threes will try to become somebody noteworthy because being a nobody is not an option. For this reason, Threes often learn to perform in ways that will garner them praise, validation and clout. We can start to catalogue the things we do that get positive reinforcement, and then put too much energy into excelling at those things.

POST PERSONALITY TEST CHECK-IN

After you've completed each test it's important to check in with yourself and assess the results. It's one thing to read them, but do they resonate with you?

What did you like the most and least about each test?

Was it easy for you to answer truthfully?

What information connected with you the most and the least?

What are three of your personality strengths and weaknesses, and were these confirmed by the tests?

Did you learn anything about yourself you didn't realise before?

Since building self-awareness is a huge reason why I've asked you to do these personality tests, I'm reminding you of some concepts from the Johari window, the starting point for our dive into personality typing. Examine all your test results and answer the following questions about your traits and behaviours.

What information did you already know about yourself and presumed that others knew too?

What information did you already know about yourself but assumed others didn't because you've hidden it?

What information have you learned about yourself that you didn't know before? What blind spots have you uncovered?

BASIC SELF-EVALUATION TASK

If you don't have access to the internet, prefer not to put this incredible book down or don't have the energy to unlock the deepest parts of your psyche with an online test, I've got an alternative for you. This is an evaluation you can do alone or with company. Simply answer these prompts and prepare to be wowed at how much you do or don't know about yourself.

1. I wish people would talk more about ...

2. I wish people would talk less about ...

3. When I feel hurt, I ...

4. When I'm annoyed, I have a tendency to ...

5. I feel accomplished when I ...

6. I feel like I've failed when I ...

How you answer can reveal a lot about what you fear and crave, which in turn can tell you what some of your motivations or hidden barriers might be.

Why we should talk about your **FLAWS**

Caution: reading this section might be a downer. After all, who wants to talk about their imperfections? This girl and people who understand that you won't discover the real you by yelling, 'I'm worthy of abundance and goodness' in the mirror until you believe it.

Flaws are often defined as an undesirable quality in a person. It's a shortcoming, an insecurity, a limitation, a deficiency, a phobia, a neurosis or a problem that affects the way we behave or how we're perceived. Flaws can alter how you feel about your personality, your life, your looks, your output or your future. Our flaws can be real or imagined; they can inhibit both the way you interact with other people and how others engage with you. Flaws are complex and confusing, but most of all, they're common. **Every single person has flaws, and in a lot of ways that's just what being human is about.**

Flaws are a paradoxical concept. So vague and yet so deep. Universal but circumstantial. The only truth is that how they affect you and the people around you is more important than the flaw itself. You can probably recall a time in your life when someone made you aware of a flaw and it hit you like the smell of bin juice on a hot day. Perhaps a relative told you that you were 'a lot', your teacher told you that you 'lacked follow-through', or your best friend told you that you were' 'unreliable'. While you might not have been consciously affected at the time, it's hard not to internalise negative feedback.

I don't mean to be grim or to paint flaws out to be scary monsters waiting to terrorise you, strip you of your self-esteem and leave you out in the cold; I just want you to know that I get it. But like most fears, there is a time when you need to conquer them. Not by pretending you don't have any, but by adopting a healthier way of viewing them.

Not dwelling on your flaws can definitely be a healthy coping mechanism, but optimism shouldn't always trump realism. It's important to identify and overcome difficult feelings and when you avoid them in favour of 'posi-vibes', you could risk falling into toxic positivity.

The toxic-positivity movement has been trending for a while now. It's the concept that encourages people to focus on the good and reject anything that could trigger negative emotions. **We're socialised to feel wrong if we experience anything that isn't palatable, optimistic and enjoyable — but that's just not realistic.** That behaviour makes us feel guilty, which then causes us to start scrambling for solutions to mask or delete that negativity ASAP. When we can't, we add to this continuous cycle of shame. We suppress our true selves, then catastrophise about how we'll never be happy, calm or rational enough.

Here's an example of how toxic positivity manifests in language. By recognising what this looks like you can start to adjust how you speak, then, by proxy, how you respond.

SITUATION	POSITIVITY	TOXIC POSITIVITY
You yelled at your housemate for eating your food without asking you or replacing it.	It's pretty normal to react like you did. Yes, it was a little aggressive, but that situation was hectic!	Stop being so negative! Only give love not hate. There's more than enough to go around and I'm sure they needed it.
You've tried to have a constructive conversation with your boss about how you're stressed and feeling unsupported at work. They keep minimising your feelings, all the while telling you that you're doing great.	It's so awesome that you were able to recognise how you're feeling and to confront your boss. You should be proud of yourself even if you didn't get the response you wanted.	Be grateful! It could be worse. Some people don't even have jobs.
Your two best friends are having a huge fight and want you to mediate it. You think they're both in the wrong, but don't want to tell them that and risk them getting mad at you.	This is a really hard situation. You're capable and will do what you think is best. Your friends love you and should respect your decision no matter what.	You're so lucky to have friends who trust you to help them. You should be grateful and look on the bright side.

Contrary to popular belief, suppressing the bad stuff doesn't really work. **If you don't give your problem areas the attention they deserve, they don't disappear.** Our anxiety feeds these areas and they develop into a baby of bad vibes that gobbles up your insecurities, then grows into a fully fledged, emotionally chaotic adult. OK, that's dramatic. REWIND.

When we gloss over our less-than-savoury qualities, it becomes difficult to make honest and open assessments of ourselves. I'm not saying you always have to love your flaws, but I'm encouraging you to get to know them on a personal level.

Wine, dine and woo your flaws – that's real self-care.

When you acknowledge your reality, it helps you to consciously choose your next step. Let's stop being passive participants in our lives and start being active ones. Let's validate all the parts of ourselves, not just the ones that are chill, agreeable and easy to accommodate. It takes a lot of courage, but you'll be better for it.

NOT ALL FLAWS ARE MADE THE SAME

Some will ruin your life (overdramatic!), some don't really matter, and others are so endearing that you'll be considered absolutely normal with just a hint of quirky. Similar to the Johari window, flaws can be broken down into four loose categories:

Things about you that are known to you and others.

Things about you that are known to you and not others.

Things about you that are unknown to you but known to others.

Things about you that are unknown to both you and others.

I'd also like to make the distinction between a circumstantial flaw and a character flaw.

Circumstantial flaws are:

Often situational.

Generally triggered by your environment.

Often the result of something that's happened to you.

Usually not a reflection of you as a person and are more likely to just be bad-habit building.

I struggle to consistently do things that I know are good for me: to be healthy, eat well, arrange and attend doctors' appointments, exercise, drink enough water or sleep the 'right' amount (it's always too little or too much). These are my circumstantial flaws, and while they don't make me a bad person, they absolutely affect me negatively and I'd benefit from fixing them.

Character flaws are:

Personality or behavioural quirks that are inherent to you and not necessarily triggered by an event.

A reflection of you as a person and your character.

Traits that impact who you are, how you act and how you respond.

The result of nature or nurture.

I'm very moody and temperamental, which means that how I respond to stimuli is primarily impacted by how I'm feeling rather than what is going on. So, on a day when I'm particularly spiky, even a relatively nice interaction can rub me the wrong way. *Did that guy say hello in a condescending tone or am I simply having a moment?*

Defining character flaws as a weakness would be an oversimplification. We need to stop automatically presuming that flaws are negative. Flaws are incredibly diverse, they can be anything from imperfections to vices, phobias to bad habits, or on a more extreme scale, they can be prejudices.

As we discuss this topic, I want you to put more focus on how you view your flaws in relation to yourself, as opposed to how you think others might view them. However, considering how your flaws could be perceived externally can be a way to develop your self-awareness and increase the area of yourself that is known.

Flaws can be separated into three key categories:

1. *Minor flaw* — These are slight imperfections, which are ultimately inconsequential to you. Neither changing a minor flaw or staying the same would improve or detract from your life. These flaws are closer to quirks and might even be the thing which makes you more memorable. When minor flaws are referenced in literature, they're defined as imperfections that make you distinguishable from other characters in the mind of the person reading the book. It could be something as simple as cracking your knuckles, twirling your hair or saying 'like' a lot in conversation. Mine could be that I excessively use exclamation marks!!!!

2. *Major flaw* — As the name suggests, these are usually more noticeable than a minor flaw, and because of that a major flaw can be limiting to you in some way. The issue with a major flaw is not what it is, but how it impacts what you do, why you do it, and

your perception of the world. They could manifest as a limiting personal-belief like self-deprecation or seeing your flaws as who you are rather than what you do, for example saying 'I'm a very temperamental person' rather than 'I have temperamental moods'. **It is up to you to assess and identify what your major flaw is, so you can soon address how it affects you.** You may not be able to change it, but at this point understanding is the bigger priority.

3. *Fatal flaw* — Academics say the fatal flaw is what causes an exceptionally great character to bring about their own downfall and, often, their eventual death. That definition is very extra, and not the energy I want to bring into this space.

To me, your fatal flaw can be defined as your Achilles heel. It's the trait or behaviour you have that consistently causes trouble. That being said, you don't necessarily want to delete this flaw from your life because it can also be something that helps you. The trick is to learn how to manage it.

My fatal flaw is that I'm a scatterbrained, big-picture person. I'm constantly jumping from tab to tab, idea to idea, project to project. I can't (or don't want to) focus on one thing at a time. This can be an issue for me as success requires concentration and often single-mindedness. But despite this, my fatal flaw has given me the gift of objectivity and the ability to troubleshoot. Because I'm always thinking about better ways to approach everything I do, my flaw helps me to look at things from different angles and pick them apart.

BLINDSPOT FLAWS

You will never be able to experience yourself the way other people do. You won't ever truly know how people see you, what they think about you or which parts of yourself are unconsciously impacting how you're perceived. It's naive to think that we have the scope to understand exactly how others see us.

When we did the Johari window activity, we talked about the areas of your personality that are known to others and unknown to you. The reason we're focusing on making these unknown areas more obvious is to increase our level of self-awareness. We don't know what we don't know. For this exercise, I want you to find some external feedback on what your flaws are. It's great to ask your close friends, family and colleagues for feedback, but beware, not all feedback is the right feedback, and many people are biased in how they interpret us as people. This means there are heaps of people who it's better not to ask. They include:

People who love you unconditionally. When it comes to you, they have their rose-coloured glasses on 25/8. It's endearing and sweet to know that there are people who see the best in you no matter what, but for the purpose of this exercise we need people who are comfortable with giving you constructive criticism.

Savage people who love you unconditionally, also known as 'tough lovers'. Like those who love you unconditionally, these people want the best for you and prioritise getting the message across instead of being tactful. In delivering their feedback, they might forget that words can be weapons and may unknowingly hurl abuse disguised as constructive criticism.

People who are scared to hurt your feelings. They prefer to prioritise the comfort of both parties, which is so lovely, but not the best approach to an exercise that requires intense truth-telling. It's not that truth and discomfort go hand-in-hand, but in this instance they might.

People who you haven't been your 'true self' around. This one is super important. If you've been withholding parts of yourself consciously, playing a character or trying to appear differently than usual around these people, they are not the ones you can trust with critical feedback. They don't see the full picture.

Party friends! Not everyone will have these types of friendships, but I define them as the people you're happy to share laughs and gossip with (generally in the context of a party), but in your day-to-day life you likely wouldn't consider them a true friend. Think of these people as acquaintances who create the illusion of feeling closer to you than they are. These surface friends haven't yet seen all your layers and that's likely because you don't feel comfortable exposing your inner self to them, and even if you did, they wouldn't know you well enough to evaluate you critically.

People who won't tell you that you have food in your teeth, toilet paper on your shoe, a wet booger clinging to your nose or period-stained jeans.

People who you should ask include:

Someone who understands why you're interested in uncovering more about yourself. They could also be on a self-development journey or are naturally intuitive and in touch with themselves. If someone doesn't see the point in why you're seeking out this information, then how will they know what is the most important feedback to give you?

Someone who knows you well. You could be acquainted for five years or five months — time isn't the only measure of connection. You know when you know.

Someone who admires you and has seen you make mistakes. They have the range to see you as both human and superhuman. We need this duality.

Someone discerning enough to see the difference between occasional poor behaviour or continuous personality flaws.

Someone who can articulately explain to you what they're interpreting from your flaw.

After you've sifted through everyone you know and applied this vigorous eligibility criteria, you should be left with around three people. Proceed with caution. **The person you ask about your flaws shouldn't be your answer to Oprah, nor should they be roleplaying as your psychologist.** They're simply there to provide insight into what the flaw is, not to theorise why you have it. We don't have time to be triggered by overzealous loved ones. We're here to extract information, ruminate over it, draw conclusions, unlock parts of our behaviour that were once unknown and then move onto the next chapter.

The right person for the job should help you with clarity. If their observations make you feel defensive, resist the urge to unleash and just know it's all part of the bigger picture.

WHAT

IS

YOUR

FATAL

FLAW?

We discussed what fatal flaws are (in the context of this book, not the over-the-top literary example of what will kill you) and now we need to uncover what yours is. What behaviour do you have that consistently causes trouble? What's the trait that some might perceive as a negative or your weakness?

Perhaps your fatal flaw is that you're scared of rejection. It's a pretty universal and common experience, which results in a lot of people being scared of putting themselves out there. They'd prefer to stay in situations that are comfortable and familiar, even if they're not necessarily healthy, productive or constructive. Sometimes being scared of rejection can lead to feeling stagnant. Trying something new or uncertain can leave you metaphorically paralysed, stopping you from progressing in a lot of ways.

In the early stages of uncovering the 'real you', you might come across some personality traits that you hate. Ones that you've only noticed in extreme cases, or others which you hadn't considered to be an issue until you read about how they can impact you negatively. Maybe you've never actually thought about your 'problem' areas at length before, and this revelation is slightly troubling to you. That's OK, everyone has parts of themselves they don't love. **When building self-awareness, don't feel pressure to eradicate the parts that make you human.** Your job is just to get a better grasp on who you are. After all, you are the sum of all your good, neutral and bad bits. The trick is to try not to hate those traits so much you wish that they didn't exist; channel that energy into curiosity and instead learn how to make these parts of yourself work in your favour.

TASK

WHAT ARE YOUR FLAWS?

Here's where we put all that knowledge into practice. Understanding what defines a flaw is just the first step; the next is coming to terms with what yours are.

1. What are your circumstantial flaws?

2. How do you think you developed your circumstantial flaw?

3. What are your minor character flaws?

4. What are your major character flaws?

5. What is your fatal flaw?

6. Do you feel like you can use your fatal flaw to your advantage? How?

7. Can you recall a time when your flaw got in the way of success? What happened and how did you manage it? If the situation arose again, how would you handle it differently?

WHAT NOW?

As I've reiterated in a thousand different ways, the solution isn't to eliminate your fatal flaw. It's probably an integral part of you and getting rid of it could trigger a huge and deadly butterfly effect. Instead, ask yourself, how can I turn this potential setback into an advantage? How can I minimise the disadvantages?

Considering you've lived with this fatal flaw your whole life and turned out OK, you may be wondering what the incentive is to change. Ignoring your flaws has worked just fine so far. Honestly, you could probably go about your life making zero changes and be pretty effective at doing what you do. But you've picked up this book for a reason, and now you're officially in the middle of an experiment and owe it to yourself to see it through.

I know that I'm terrible at making sure that I get enough sleep, so I tell people, 'I'm trying to sleep earlier. Hold me accountable.' I know that I'm also terrible at drinking enough water, but I let people around me know that's a concern for me and ask them to help me meet my goals. **It's really important to keep people cognisant of the journey that you're on, so when you're slipping and unaware that you are doing so, it's easier to nip it in the bud and turn that around.**

YOU KNOW WHO ARE NOW

You're ever-changing as a human, so you'll never entirely know who you are (remember the blind self?) but you know more about yourself than you did before you started reading, and that's incredible.

Reminder: It can be hard to keep on track and avoid regressing into your former self or performing because it's easier than growing. The reason you've agreed to this experiment is because you want to work on yourself. You want to evolve. You want to be better. Don't forget yourself.

If you find yourself slipping back, just read through the book again as a refresher. Spend extra time on the bits that really resonated with and inspired you, and look back on the exercises you've completed, paying close attention to how your results may have shifted. There is no rush to move on to the next chapters if you're not ready; the experiment will wait for you.

STEP TWO

Know

you

to

CHAPTER TWO

who want be

WHAT THIS CHAPTER *WILL* TEACH YOU

Wanting to evolve doesn't mean you dislike yourself

How to do a self-SWOT analysis

What you and the iPhone have in common

The difference between thriving and surviving (Spoiler: it has nothing to with being on a desert island and only being able to bring three things)

How to create a healthy narrative about who you want to become

The importance of gratitude, affirmations and mantras

The difference between what you actually want and what you tell people you want

TWO

The path to success is a wobbly mess

How abundant thinking will help you improve your perspective

How to conquer your subconscious mind

WHAT THIS CHAPTER *WON'T* TEACH YOU

How to forget who you actually are

How to become a caricature of yourself

How to convince yourself that you can't improve

How to set unrealistic expectations of the person you want to be

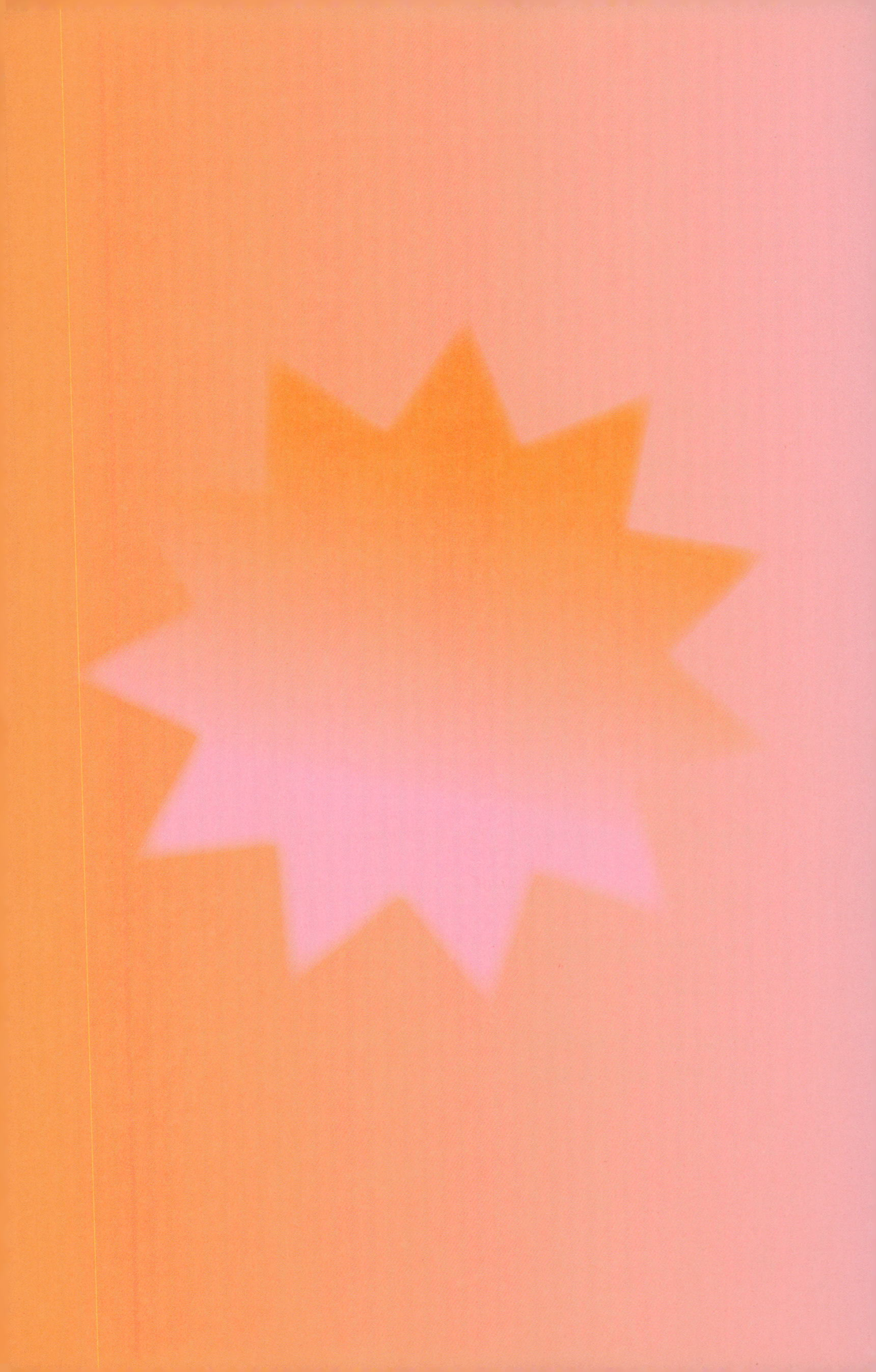

Presuming that you're reading this book in chronological order, you've probably just spent some time dissecting yourself. Who are you? Why are you this way? What's informed the way you see yourself and how do others see you? What are your strengths and weaknesses? And of course, the big wildcard, what are your blind spots? As you know, this is a book about conducting an experiment to see if you can achieve success using the method I've created, based on analysing my own experience in hindsight. It may feel like all this talk about self-reflection, introspection and evaluation are just the primer in the lead-up to The Big Experiment, but no, everything you're reading now is an integral part of the bigger picture. **Repeat after me: this is the experiment**. It's important you soak up all the details in every section you read, because they will give you the skills necessary to get the most out what's to come.

After reading the last chapter you're probably hyperaware of all the things you like about your behaviour and a lot of things you may want to improve on. Heck, you're probably fantasising about what life would be like if you were your best self (no, just me?) or, even better, what changes you could make now which would get you closer to evolving and becoming a better version of you.

Knowing that there are areas you need to work on will feel exponentially different for every individual. You might feel insecure about not being a finished product or anxious that you don't have enough time to change. You might feel avoidant, preferring to focus on the good areas of your personality and not the ones you regard as bad, or you could still be processing how you feel. Personally, I get excited at the thought of knowing that I can be better because I've always been in environments where improving has been encouraged and praised. Satiating my curiosity and learning new things is a big yes for me. It fulfils my need to be validated, and you already know I love recognition. Give me my props, I say!

This brings us to our next step. Nip-tucking and tweaking ourselves to uncover who we want to be. If alarm bells are sounding, quieten them. **Please don't misinterpret knowing what you want to be with ridding yourself of all the traits and quirks that make you, you.** I'm also not advocating that you strip yourself down to the bare bones until you're a blank canvas. And I'm definitely not encouraging you to mould yourself into a carbon copy of what you think success looks like, especially if those traits are nothing like your own. In my few orbits around the sun I've been inundated with models for what successful people do and how they should think, look and act, and that's made me want to mimic them, disregarding how that contradicts what I actually want. It's pretty likely that you've adopted these attitudes, as well. Going to university and accumulating debt, regardless of the fact you didn't know what you wanted to do, because of internal and external pressure. Dating someone who looked good on paper despite the fact that they weren't the best partner for you, because being in a relationship is considered aspirational by many. Conforming and wearing specific clothing or makeup in professional environments, not because you felt comfortable doing so, but because you presumed it was an expectation. We've all been there, I know it's not just me!

As we go through this experiment, we're going to spend a lot of time making the distinction between what we think we want, what we actually want, what we feel pressured to want and what we've been programmed or conditioned to want. It would be counterintuitive not to unpack the idea that we might really not even want success of any kind, but we often aren't given room to explore the alternative.

I'm not saying that this is your experience, but it's a common enough way of thinking that's worth mentioning. In life, there are heaps of instances where we choose to do what's been done before because it's easy, more accessible or we perceive it to have a higher success rate. We become so outcome-oriented and goal-driven that we forget we have the option to dream of things outside of the norm. We follow the road frequently travelled because it can feel like we're running out of time; we prioritise getting to our destination quickly so we can say we did something. This is how we get sucked into a cycle of validation through any means necessary.

We're constantly reminded that we won't be this young, smart, carefree, time-rich, open-minded or hopeful forever, because life is going to wear us down. **To avoid the uncertainty and the stress that comes with not doing 'the Thing', we follow the unwritten guideline of how to do life properly.** We get the traditional job, date the realistic person, live in the accessible places in the hopes that if we get the foundation of our lives figured out quickly, we can finally do the things we actually want to do.

But how many times have we seen that strategy work? Rarely, sometimes, frequently? I don't know what your experience has been like, but I do know that the blueprints of the lives around you can impact how you've chosen to live your own. If you've seen people you know go down the traditional-success route and enjoy it, that could be your reference point. If you've seen people try something new and not get their desired outcome, that could deter you from doing the same. I'm not saying that either method is good, bad, right, wrong, effective or ineffective. I'm just pointing out that we have choices (more often than we realise), and giving yourself the time and space to think about what you actually want, who you want to be and then pursuing opportunities with those in mind could have some really positive results.

Our goal in this experiment is to discover and amplify the areas of your personality that work in your favour. I don't know you personally and I don't have an all-seeing eye that's going to show me your individual traits and how to improve them, but I do have exercises that can help give you some insight.

We're not using this experiment as an excuse to rag on the 'shittier' parts of ourselves, discard them or render them useless. However, we will spend some time learning how to identify the less desirable aspects of our personalities and how to stop them from having such a negative impact. This will involve more introspection and evaluation.

We'll also dissect what image you conjure up when you think of a successful person. Not so you can try to replicate it, but so we can understand what's informed your ideas of success. From there, we'll figure out what your own model of success looks like — is it the Hollywood archetype? You know, the suit, money, formal speaking-voice, the 187-hour work week, rise-and-grind, sleep-when-you're-dead attitude? Or is it something less common? It's OK if you don't know exactly what this is yet, that's why I've written this book. **We're working towards creating a personalised, bespoke approach to success, based on your own goals, ambitions and personality. But we can't get there without figuring you out first.**

PREPARE
YOURSELF
FOR SOME
DEEP
THINKING.

CHECKPOINT

This is the point where we assess how you feel about success. This will likely change and evolve as you make your way through the experiment; but either way, if you don't understand what success means to you then you can't know what goal you're working towards.

Checking back in with yourself is not just another way to take a rest, it's a crucial part of the process, which ensures that when you're moving forward it's in the direction you actually want to go. Like I said, it's easy to get into a cycle of success by any means necessary, where we thirst for symbols of winning without caring if the prize we get is the one we'd intended. Yes, all progress is good, but is all progress right? The fact is, if you zoom forward and arrive at a destination you didn't like, you have to go backwards to get to where you need to be. This is not to be confused with regressing, but there definitely is a point where you'll have to stop, reflect and do the work you've already done again.

When I worked in social media and digital communications and made the transition from working full-time to part-time (before eventually quitting to become a DJ), I didn't have a clear definition of what success was. Because of that, I was looking for symbols of achievement to confirm that I was doing the 'right thing', which at that point was more money, more free time and more clout. I didn't really consider what the implications of uprooting myself from a stable and secure work environment to an extremely turbulent one might be. If we were going to do a self-awareness analysis on this moment in my life, it would be easy to see that the areas which were known to me were tiny and my blind spot and unknown areas were huge. I could say that I'm lucky it all worked out for me, but I'm now in a position where I'm more inclined to take calculated risks, realising how bad the blowback from my big career-decision could have been.

I didn't make my transition with any intention or strategy in place, and in retrospect that makes it hard to reflect properly on that time and see if this goal I achieved was what I wanted. Yes, I remember wanting more time, but what was I planning to do with it? Yes, I wanted more money, but was that because of security or frivolity? I can only guess.

Going forward, evolving, transforming, transitioning — these are all huge priorities. But they have to be used in conjunction with reflection and introspection. It's important to keep checking back in with yourself to ensure you're making progress, and to do that you need to be able to compare where you are to where you came from. Remember, these activities aren't single serve — no matter where you are in your success experiment you can always come back later on to see if you still feel the same way. Consider:

What does success look like to you now?

What did success look like to you five years ago?

What has influenced your perception of success?

How would you feel if you were told you'd never be successful?

What do you think you need to change about your personality, behaviour or environment to be successful?

Has learning your personality type affected who you want to be? Why?

GET TO KNOW YOUR STRENGTHS

Consider your strengths as a fail-safe superpower. Your personal strengths might not be the rarest or the most coveted skills, but they're ones you can trust yourself to use with your eyes closed (figuratively, of course). When everything's turning to shit, you should feel comfortable whipping out these tools.

It can be helpful to think about your strengths in context. For example, you could be an amazing writer who understands syntax, grammar and can turn any bland sentence into a literary masterpiece. However, in your life you're surrounded by other great wordsmiths, so it can feel like this isn't a particularly special skill but it's still an ability you have which you believe separates you from the average person. Maybe you have the patience of a saint, the palate of a Michelin star chef, or the attention to detail of a detective. If you're unsure of where your strengths lie, there's an easy activity to help you uncover them.

Grab your notebook (or open up your digital notepad, whatever you want) and answer the questions below. Reflecting on your responses will give insight into your holistic strengths as an individual, which set you apart from the rest.

What are you naturally good at?

What advantages do you have (skills, certifications, education, or connections)?

Which of your achievements are you most proud of?

What are your values or ethics, and do you believe others feel the same?

Which of your personality traits do you like the most?

Which of your traits have helped you most during your career and relationships?

What do other people (your boss, in particular) see as your strengths?

GET TO KNOW YOUR WEAKNESSES

Weaknesses are 'negative' factors that can inhibit your strengths from thriving. These are aspects of your personality that can be worth improving as a way to give you a competitive advantage in your personal and professional life. This exercise is all about uncovering the problem areas that you need to learn to manage. Ask yourself:

What are you pretty trash at?

What areas of your education could you develop further?

Do you have any traits that have caused issues in your career or relationships in the past?

What parts of your personality do you feel could be improved?

What tasks do you avoid because you don't feel comfortable doing them?

How do you normally procrastinate?

What are your negative habits and traits?

What would other people see as your weaknesses?

TIME TO

UPGRADE

There are two types of people in the world: those who rush to click 'yes' when their device offers a system upgrade, and those who ferociously ignore the notification for all eternity, later wondering why their electronics crash and die untimely deaths. Those who chose to update understand that it's extremely beneficial and can improve their quality of life (even if it means a slight halt in progress and a moment to get used to the changes). Those who ignore the upgrade probably live in fear of the unknown, plagued by what-ifs and are likely more uncomfortable with disrupting their norms, even if it the outcome would boost their lives.

This is all to say that humans are very complex and unique and, undoubtedly, we have a lot to learn about ourselves. **How we think, what we do and why we do it are all impacted by our behaviour and personality.** Something as simple as clicking a button and updating our phone software is influenced by all this underlying stuff that most of us aren't even aware of. Why do some of us delay this? Why do some of us rush? What impacts these differing choices? How conscious are we of this? How conscious *should* we be?

The answers lie within this chapter. In order to get the best results in this experiment, you need to be willing to double-click and put yourself through a system upgrade. Unlike tech software, this isn't going to be as simple as pressing a button and letting binary code do its thing; this is going to involve a constant analysis on yourself. In chapter one, we developed an understanding of your behaviour and personality; we wanted to see what you were working with. In this chapter, **we're going to learn how best to utilise who you are for the results you want.**

THRIVING vs SURVIVING

Thriving: An ideal state of being where you are consciously flourishing, growing, developing and prospering. This state can vary for different people. Although I don't have a green thumb and I definitely don't consider myself a gardener, I think of plants when people ask me to explain what it means to thrive. Some plants require a little sun, while others require lots. Some need their thirst quenched daily and others are happy with every other day. It's easy for us to comprehend that these leafy creatures need different things to be in their optimum state. Use the same line of thinking when it comes to yourself, and know that people in a thriving state will be progressing in a way that looks (and often feels) easy, effortless and natural.

In my experience, thriving is often associated with an abundance mentality: the positive mindset that there is always 'more' on its way to you. **More rest, luck, love, opportunity, time, money, energy, resources and, most definitely, more success.** When you're thriving, the thought of winning or getting your desired result is not foreign; if anything, you trust that it will happen. Not to be confused with delusion, abundant thinking is a great resilience builder — you acknowledge the reality of your situation while making proactive choices to improve it.

Surviving: This is a pretty common state of being. Simply existing, getting by and just trying to get through the day in one piece. Preferring to settle or reach for the lowest hanging fruit because it's easy, reliable and dependable. Doing what you did yesterday every day is bound to get you the same results, so what's the problem? Stagnancy is the problem. **Not moving forward or progressing means that you're evolving at a slower rate.** Getting to where you want to go takes so long that you convince yourself that it's unlikely, or worse, impossible.

From there it's easy to develop a scarcity mindset, a negative way of thinking that tells you there's never anything more or better coming your way. Less rest, luck, love, opportunity, money, energy, resources and, most definitely, less success. Instead of trying to challenge your reality, you use confirmation bias to justify why things are the way they are. You applied for one job and didn't get it, so now you think you're destined to be poor. You struggled with getting the marks needed to enter university, so you must not be smart. This mindset absolutely impacts your relationship with achievement, because if you haven't had any wins, you'll presume that there isn't enough good to go around (no matter how hard you try). This can manifest differently for everyone. **You might avoid trying because you presume the outcome will be bad or you feel like you're not worthy of success.** You could start making loose decisions, thinking that strategy won't be able to help you. Or you might just operate in a docile, sleepy state, only doing what needs to be done in the hopes that one day you'll be able to actually do what you want.

I can teach you how to avoid surviving and prioritise thriving. The first step is to make sure you really understand the differences between the two. I've popped a table below with a few examples, but like always, whip out your notebook, make your own table and populate it with information. Let it marinate and reflect on it regularly.

A PERSON SURVIVING (SCARCITY)	A PERSON THRIVING (ABUNDANCE)
Associates trying something new with risk and bad outcomes.	Associates trying something new with overwhelming positive opportunities.
Is scared to fail.	Knows that failure is just a part of the process.
Has an undercurrent of stinginess; keeps their cards close to their chest.	Sees the value in sharing.
Constantly thinks that there's not enough to go around.	Knows that there's more than enough to go around.

There's a ton of research into the science of happiness conducted by the Harvard Business Review, Safe Work Australia, the University of Warwick, Queens School of Business and positivity psychologist Martin Seligman, which suggests that when you feel happy you're more productive. The more productive you are, the quicker you'll dive headfirst into whatever experiences or projects you come across. If you can create scenarios where you're able to thrive, it becomes easier for you to transition into a more focused, productive, proactive, adaptable and resilient version of yourself.

It took me a whole lifetime (and a hundred or so pages) to explain it — happiness, purpose, wants and how they intersect with one's idea of success — but I needed us to both go on the journey together. I'm a rambler and an abstract thinker, so sometimes it takes me a second to get to the root of what I'm actually trying to convey. Despite my personal and professional achievements, I'm not always thriving, I find myself slipping back into survival mode. **It's taken a lot of broken nails, bad ideas, sweat, late nights, elaborate emails, discarded projects and tears to get to this place in my life, but there have been times it's felt so easy I would've called it good luck.** Insecurity is a friend of mine and she pops in every now and then to say hey, usually overstaying her welcome. We chat, she asks me if I ever wonder if everything will be taken from me one day. The strong, rational, resilient part of me says, 'Who's going to do that? Who has that power?' Then Miss Insecurity chips away at me until I forget I'm talented and capable. 'Anyone,' I say. Insecurity's job is done, and she goes to visit someone else, leaving me with the ramifications of our conversation. Suddenly I'm sceptical of others, fearful that they're going to take my spot, and so scared that I feel powerless. (Is it because I am, or is it just a feeling? Who knows?) I stick to the script, do what's been done, say the right things and push all the discomfort to the very bottom; hoping that if I push far enough it'll disappear, but it doesn't. Eventually I have to check in with the Lil that occupies my mind to have a D & M and find the root of the problem.

Moments of consistent distress can pull us back into juvenile versions of ourselves, which can make growth and progression feel like an uphill battle. We can't avoid these moments completely, but we can mitigate the negative effects on us by challenging them head on.

Building resilience is key. Don't forget it.

WHAT'S MY STORY?

Five years ago, I was a social media and digital communications manager. It was a good enough job in that it paid in dollars, stress and burnout, all the things I'd been told were prerequisites for a fulfilling career. Every day in that environment was a testament to the fact that money can buy you distractions from sadness, but if you don't know what actually fuels you and makes you happy, that is not a sustainable way to live.

At that point, I still hadn't realised that I wasn't inspired or motivated by the traditional representations of success. Not because the signs weren't there, but because I refused to believe that the things I pined for just weren't right for me. I think, deep down, I associated that revelation with failure, and I wasn't comfortable with that just yet. I had to remember that, above it all, I was a competitive person who valued winning, validation and recognition. My career was ticking all of those boxes in some way, so I preferred to disregard the blaring signs that were spelling out, THIS IS NOT OK AND YOU'RE NOT FULFILLED.

I attached my self-worth to the job, but I felt mediocre because I wasn't fulfilled by the work, and as a result my output was mediocre. It hadn't yet occurred to me to seek purpose from anything outside of my career, so my solution was to find a cooler job. I didn't think about the characteristics of a job description that would fulfil me. Not because I didn't care, but I already had my eyes locked onto greener pastures and had to get there quickly. If Present-Day Me was managing that situation, I would've written a list of career non-negotiables, then started searching with that in mind. I would've found a role where I could flex my creative muscles, work autonomously and have authority (but not have to manage anyone), all in a place where I could wear what I want and have an easy commute.

Past Me was not that switched on. Past Me just fell into a shiny opportunity, put all her eggs in one basket and didn't look back. Fortunately for Past Me, I was smart enough not to quit my job and forgo all of my security, so I dropped down to part-time to give me the space for new opportunities.

I thought I'd do productive things with that extra day off, but I didn't. I did, however become a club doorbitch for two or three nights of the week, which then transitioned into me becoming a sometimes-DJ, to quitting my day-job and DJing full-time. In retrospect, how I manoeuvred this career change is honestly secondary to why I did it. At the time, being a DJ seemed like my golden ticket as it offered me a number of awesome things.

1. *Creative outlet.* My job was to find new music (which I was already doing), get dressed up and waddle to the club on the weekends (which was perfect, considering my friends were going to be there) to play the music I like.

2. *Access to* additional resources. Building relationships with the club meant that I could borrow their equipment to practise. Surprisingly, DJing was an incredible networking opportunity. Who would've thought that all the talking I did would be so integral — I was chatting to people who would hire me in the future, recommend me to others and vouch for me and my career. My network of friends also expanded quickly to include more people working in creative fields.

3. *Flexibility. Transitioning* from just a club DJ to one who played at daytime events, festivals and for corporations meant that suddenly I had more time to do other things. I was no longer bound by the nine to five.

4. *Increased income.* The average hourly rate was much higher than my office job, so when I got bored of working less and ramped up to 35-hour weeks, it began to add up. I was building a lavish lifestyle with less hours at work.

With all these pros, there are just as many cons (which I won't get into because this book isn't about how to become a DJ.) All of these perks seemed ideal, initially, but after mere months that very familiar feeling of burnout started to creep its way back into my life. All the evaluation I didn't do before I made the career jump was starting to backfire on me. I wasn't feeling as fulfilled, motivated or as present as I'd imagined. How was this even possible? I had completed my goal — I got out of the old, boring job and into a new, fun one — but still I felt the same.

I couldn't understand what was happening and why I wasn't able to regulate the way I was feeling. I was surviving, not thriving, and chose to make a huge life decision based on my superficial ideals, without any critical thinking. Looking back, I love that I thought it was my inability to regulate my emotions that was the problem and not my lack of self-awareness. **I told myself that I was unhappy because I probably didn't know how to see happiness properly.** I thought I was just having a moment and that balance would be restored eventually if I just sat tight and let life do its thing. After months of flip-flopping between feeling lucky to have a creative job and begrudgingly waddling to said job, I had what I can only describe as an epiphany. I had constructed a narrative in my head about what I wanted my career to be, and that wasn't aligning with the reality of my experience. I had to remind myself that becoming a DJ was never actually what I wanted. Not entirely, anyway. I wanted a cooler job, and to feel grateful, alive, excited and creative. I wanted to know that I was good at what I was doing.

This! ^^^ Could! Be! Any! Job! Or! Experience!

When the opportunity to DJ came along, I clung to it so hard to that I didn't give myself a chance to properly consider it. But who wouldn't?! You saw my list of perks. I still think DJing is the coolest job ever, despite it not being the right fit for me. Buckets of introspection showed me a few things that I knew for sure:

I didn't want to work in a structured environment.

I didn't want what I wore to be dictated by anyone else but me. No dress code, please! Can we dead the narrative that people who add a bit of flavour to their outfits are less capable than those who don't?

I wanted to be gratified and validated for being myself.

I wanted to make more money.

I wanted to be an entrepreneur and an authority figure.

I wanted to express myself freely through my personality and creativity.

I wanted to work in environments where my tastes and opinion were appreciated.

I wanted to work to timelines that I chose.

I wanted education and learning to be a prerequisite to my work.

I wanted to continue to evolve and grow as a person.

Yes, all of those things intersected with DJing, but they also intersect with a hundred other career paths and life activities ... If I was focusing on the characteristics of what success looks like to me (as opposed to trying to consolidate it into a neat title) I could've dodged months of clinical exhaustion, as well as the stress of disregarding how I felt to make it look like everything was fine. This all sounds dramatic, but I think that's only because I put a lot of pressure on myself to do things right ('right' is circumstantial, I know), so when I think I've haven't done things properly I freak out. I don't recall what my main fear was — perhaps admitting that I thought I'd made a mistake or that my dream job wasn't that dreamy. It might even have been as simple as not having a Plan B and feeling trapped.

Scarcity mindset really took a hold of me during this time. It was almost like I thought I had no choices and I was stuck between a rock and a hard place, when really, I just had to take the time to think, analyse and make a decision.

What I've learned is that sometimes attaching your wants and needs to a rigid goal (like career, a partner, moving to a new city, starting a business, breaking a world record, etc.) can actually distract you from your real motivators. This is why figuring out your feelings, traits or ideas of success is one of the most important steps in determining what you want to do and who you want to be. **Find your motivators, know your strengths and use these to create a goal that's suited to you.** You can still want the car, holiday, business or hobby, but how you achieve those things needs to be tailored to you.

This experiment is about you, not me, so I want to invite you to think selfishly about what you want. Think literally, laterally, superficially, genuinely and abundantly. Don't limit yourself; no matter how outlandish your ambition is, it's better to cast a net wide and then allow yourself to zero in on specifics as you learn and grow.

Perhaps you want:

A chance to explore a new place and experience different cultures.

To put yourself out there and be a little uncomfortable, to encourage growth.

To meet new people.

An incentive to start living life differently.

Time off work.

We're not all the same and it's likely you want something completely different. I'm asking you to invest in yourself, take however much time you need, whip out your notebook and write down exactly what your aspirations are. Aim for a list of ten. They don't have to be grand or special, they just have to be yours.

Think selfishly about what you want.

WHAT'S YOUR STORY?

Most successful people have 'a story' — a tale they tell an audience of adoring fans or sceptics; a journey that puts their growth into perspective, justifies their accomplishments and motivates listeners to keep pushing forward on their own paths.

Since you're at the beginning of your own story, it's not unusual that you don't have a Nobel Prize-winning piece of non-fiction ready to go — so we're going to work backwards to create a narrative of who you want to become, taking into consideration who you are now. You might not have a good idea of what you want just yet, but we're not here for specifics — this is where we brainstorm.

The best advice I can give you right now is to chase the idea of what your future could be. Think about all the possibilities as opposed to one stringent title. When you chase an idea, you can do so knowing it's fluid, malleable, resilient and subject to change. When you chase a title, it's fixed, rigid and sometimes leaves you little room to evaluate the goal until you've reached it.

If you're still not quite grasping the difference between title and idea, here are some examples:

I want a long-term partner (title) versus I want someone I can be sexually intimate with, be vulnerable with and share new experiences with (idea).

I want to be an influencer (title) versus I want a job that lets me flex my creativity and gives me room to live my life (idea).

The questions you should ask yourself to help construct your tale for the ages are:

Who do I want to be after I finish reading this book?

What do I want to learn from this book?

How do I want to feel after reading this book?

What does success look like to me right now?

How do I want people to perceive me when I'm successful?

What will I do after I've achieved success?

What are the best and worst possible things that could happen to me after reading this book?

Now write every single thing down, no matter how basic or unfinished the thought might feel. Avoid the temptation to embellish or hide parts of yourself; we're simply using this as a foundation to help you clearly see your own vision for a more ideal you.

WHAT'S THEIR STORY?

Naturally, there is more to the world than my story and yours. I mean, considering there are almost eight billion people in the world, you'd hope so! If you're still struggling to construct an ideal narrative of the kind of person you want to be, you can start working from a blueprint of people that already exist. Why start from scratch when you don't have to?

Step one: I challenge you to think of at least five people who encompass your ideas of success. These people don't need to be similar to each other in any way, but you do need to be familiar with them and their stories.

Step two: List five things you like about each of those people. It could be their career trajectory or ability to taste-make. Or perhaps you like the way they deal with conflict, or even the way in which they're transparent about their failures.

WHAT'S THE DEAL WITH MANTRAS AND AFFIRMATIONS?

I know my value.

I'm interesting and interested.

I'm inspired and I inspire.

I have an abundance of energy.

I'm blessed and highly favoured.

If it's meant to be mine, it will be.

Success will find me today.

I excel in all that I do and success comes to me easily.

Everything I do today brings me closer to achieving my goals tomorrow.

I'm heard and understood.

I will embrace change.

I understand failure is a necessary chapter of success.

'Every day I learn more and more about myself. With each interaction I have with somebody new, I understand more about me.'

I'd be lying if I said mantras and affirmations were my thing. Out of all the ways I've chosen to exercise self-care I've put up walls of resistance to this one.

I guess I've been put off by the idea of standing in front of a mirror and telling myself I was beautiful or worthy. But, as with all things, I just had to find a way that worked for me; by that, I mean shouting in the mirror is optional.

Self-development books often talk about how legit and powerful positive affirmations are, with many big names (Oprah, especially) claiming affirmations to be a big part of their practice.

For those of you who are a little lost, here's a crash course. **To affirm is to offer emotional support or encouragement.** Translation: saying nice things to a person (or yourself) when needed. The affirmation is the word or phrase you actually use.

The origin of mantra is to chant religious phrases or repetitive sacred sounds, words or names.

Mainstream media often refers to a mantra as a phrase you choose to motivate and inspire you. It's a feel-good statement that you repeat to yourself to focus your mind and train yourself to think more positive thoughts, while encouraging a better mindset. Basically, mantras are tools that help you keep your eye on the prize.

The two phrases often get lumped into one or used interchangeably. To avoid confusion, I'll only be referencing affirmation in this book. Whether or not affirmations work has been a topic of much contention but, believe it or not, there is a genuine theory and scientific plausibility behind the practice. Let's get into it.

OK, BUT WHAT ARE POSITIVE AFFIRMATIONS?

Positive affirmations are phrases or statements used continually as a means to challenge negative or unhelpful thoughts. Whereas plain-old affirmations are more reactive and random.

Choosing a phrase to recite can be super simple. All you need to do is think of a situation in which you need a bit of a morale boost, pick a phrase that will help you keep positivity front of mind and then repeat it to yourself frequently (preferably aloud and alone). You'll know it's working when you no longer feel that slight tinge of discomfort when you repeat the affirmation.

In addition to giving yourself some extra pep in your step, affirmations can also be used to help with:

Motivation and accountability — For all the times you wish you had a direct-yet-nurturing bootcamp coach in your ear. Be your own cheerleader! Your thoughts can and will affect your life whether you like it or not, you might as well make them positive.

Goal reinforcement — It's easy to tell yourself you want to be better, get wrapped up in the narrative of doing something good for yourself and then forget to action all those positive changes. Don't worry, it happens to the best of us. Affirmations are a great way to remind yourself that it takes more than one try to get the work done.

Happiness hack — Heaps of studies have shown that people who practise positive affirmations are happier, more optimistic and have a clearer perspective on life. Turns out life is better when you whisper sweet nothings in your own ears.

Muscle-memory boost — Arguably the best way to learn and improve is through practice and repetition; positive affirmations are no exception to this rule.

Affirmations can be hard and awkward to start, especially if you find that, like me, this isn't a concept that naturally resonates with you. Some of the best advice I've been told about affirmations is to fake it till you make it. Say something before you mean it and eventually you will believe it.

WHY SHOULD I RECITE POSITIVE AFFIRMATIONS?

All of us have an inner critic who knows just how to make us feel shit, but what most of us don't have is a mental hype-man to make us feel better. That's where affirmations come in. They're a free, painless and simple way to improve your life. Generally, people use affirmations to motivate themselves, boost self-esteem, rejig their perspective and encourage positive change. But most importantly, they're made to remind us of pre-existing truths that aren't celebrated enough. It's so easy to get caught up in negative self-talk: I suck at this, OMG I never take good photos, why am I so bad at everything? You might believe these negative things to be true, or you could just be in the habit of rampant (humorous but sometimes serious) self-deprecation.

When we're feeling down, triggered or lacking, the practice of affirmation can remind us that how we feel isn't always who we are. You can be feeling stressed and not be a stress-head, just like how you can feel angry and not be an angry person. By frequently reminding ourselves of our worth, it can be easier to bounce back when we're feeling down.

Try it, you literally have nothing to lose.

THINK OF
AFFIRMATIONS AS
PSYCHOLOGICAL
GREEN JUICE.
DRENCH YOUR
MIND IN SOME
GOOD THOUGHTS
AND GET EXCITED
ABOUT THE
PERSON YOU ARE.

DOES IT ACTUALLY WORK?

Yes, but it's not completely straightforward. There's the pseudo-sciencey rationale and the super-sciencey rationale.

Scientific journal *Social Cognitive and Affective Neuroscience* published the results of a study conducted by psychologist Christopher Cascio from the University of Pennsylvania, to see if giving yourself a little verbal TLC has any actual positive results. They used brain-imaging to track activity to observe if there were any patterns consistent between all subjects who practised affirmations. In the end, they found 'novel evidence' that recurring self-affirmation can improve your sense of self and help you respond better to threats. What you personally consider to be a threat can vary wildly depending on the circumstance, but it's my understanding that a threat is anything that you'd instinctively respond poorly to.

Now, on the other end of the spectrum, let's talk New Agey spiritual affirmations. I personally think the concept has a logical foundation, but it requires a lot of intuition.

Science tells us that everything in the world is made up of atoms, which contain energy. Science also tells us that all things are constantly vibrating, even the stuff that looks like it's not moving. This means you, the floor, your car, house, light fixtures, and everything else are all a doing a little cosmic-shake, zooming too fast for your eyes to see. This movement can happen in a ton of different patterns and speeds. If something is moving slowly, it's considered to be on a lower frequency; something moving more rapidly is on a higher frequency. All these vibrations are constantly orbiting and oscillating, en route to meet something else to sync up with. Atoms attract each other so, on occasion, when various vibrating things move close to each other they can start to sync up and move together harmoniously, which means they're now operating on the same frequency.

So, let's take this concept and apply it to affirmations. Imagine that a positive or negative thought worked in the same way as an atom.

Knowing that atoms attract atoms, imagine that atom as a thought, behaviour, intention, object or experience. Be they positive or negative, those thoughts would attract counterparts travelling on the same frequency. It's said that 'good' things have a high vibration while 'bad' things have a low vibration. **The theory is that by saying sweet nothings to yourself often enough you'll increase your vibration, which is meant to shimmy you closer to positive outcomes on the same frequency as you.**

Claude Mason Steele is a social psychologist who in 1988 popularised the idea of self-affirmation. This concept suggests that we can improve our sense of self if we consistently speak to ourselves in a more positive way. Steele also said that by using self-affirming practices, we're less likely to feel insecure if someone comes at us sideways or confronts us with information that threatens our self-esteem.

Basically, what Steele's theory tells us is that the more you say nice things to or about yourself, the better you're going to feel. The better you feel, the more likely you are to act in ways that benefit you. You might start sleeping more, increase your productivity, be more personable or simply just improve your outlook on life. When you're in this upgraded state-of-mind you'll inevitably feel more secure, so if someone were to tell you that you were lazy, slow or prickly, you might not rush to get as defensive as you would have in the past.

This theory of self-affirmation has gotten heaps of clout since its inception, which has led to a lot of legit research investigating whether we can see any clear, positive changes in the brain as a result of these practices. As it turns out there is MRI evidence from Psychologist Christopher Cascio (the same person I mentioned earlier), which says that self-affirming practices activate a place in your brain that registers rewards and praise. This is the same place that gets triggered (in a good way) when we do other pleasurable stuff, like eating hot chips, receiving validation from someone you admire or looking in your bank account and realising you have more money than anticipated. Saying nice things to yourself feels good and encourages you to do good. When you act on these positive feelings you feel better in return, and the cycle of good vibes continues.

Studies have also suggested that the practice of self-affirmation is more effective when you think about your future as opposed to your past. For example, a phrase like, 'Think about all the love coming my way' will result in more positive brain activity than retrospectively thinking, 'Think about the love I've experienced'.

Researchers at the Mayo Clinic, a US non-profit academic medical centre, have also conducted studies to explore the effects that positive thinking and a generally optimistic attitude can have on your mental health. They deduced that health benefits may include living longer, lowered rates of depression, immunity boosting (including increased resistance to the common cold!!), better psychological wellbeing and more effective coping mechanisms. What's interesting is that they haven't actually figured out what it is about positive thinking that does all this good shit for you, but they have a theory that it relaxes you and a state of bliss means that you're not putting unnecessary pressure on yourself. I love it.

HOW DO I DO IT?

Honestly, affirmations can be done in whatever way feels most comfortable for you. **You can try writing them down, saying them out loud or, my personal favourite, thinking them in your head — it's private and you can do it anywhere.** Whether you're conscious of it or not, you already talk to yourself all the time. You sing songs, bully yourself, roleplay conversations that never happened and practise fake acceptance speeches.

As we've already learned, our brains can't tell the difference between reality and fantasy. Once we acknowledge that fact, we need to take it as a reminder to spend conscious time feeding our mind positive nutrients. These nutrients can come in the form of compliments, mantras and positive affirmations. Feeding our brain this positivity has so many positive outcomes, but in this chapter, we'll be using this practice to visualise the person we want to be. As I've said before, affirmations historically haven't been my thing, but thinking of this practice as mental green juice has helped me develop a few tips for using affirmations to curate a more positive mindset. Affirmations with a spiritual focus will often tell you to speak your ideal life into existence by using phrases like 'I'm in a loving relationship', when you're single, or 'I have a million dollars in the bank', when you've just over-drafted your account, again. Personally, I've found it's more helpful to focus on changing your mindset rather than making such sweeping statements. Here are a few examples to get you started:

'I can learn something from every situation.'

'I will survive this.'

'I'm learning to love myself.'

'I deserve better.'

HOT TIPS ON POSITIVE THINKING

Manifesting and positive affirmations are big ideas and, as we've discovered, the best practice can be different for everyone. To understand how these ways of thinking can be most effective for you, it's important to wrap your head around all the nitty-gritty. Luckily, I've done the leg work and put together some of the big things you should know before you start work on changing your mindset.

If positive thinking is a challenging habit for you to adopt, try learning how to minimise your negative thinking through recognising your own individual cognitive distortions. This concept was popularised in the eighties by a psychologist called David Burns. He said that there are heaps of ways your mind amplifies inaccurate (often harmful) thoughts to convince you of things that aren't true. As you check yourself and become aware of these thought patterns, it's theorised that the negative thoughts will go away over time and be replaced with more balanced ones. Then you're left with a better foundation to start practising positive thinking. Negative thought patterns can include:

Polarising — also known as black and white thinking. This is when you can only see things in binary — good or bad, win or lose, right or wrong — rather than seeing the nuance of a situation. Observing yourself or the world in this very extreme and absolute way can warp your sense of reality, making you feel like you have no opportunity to experience a better outcome.
I made a mistake at work today, so I'm bad at my job.
I've had three break-ups, which means I've had three failed relationships.

Personalising — when something bad happens, you automatically think it's your fault, even when you have no logical reason to. You jump to the conclusion that the reason for things happening is because of your inadequacy, rather than comprehending that not everything is within your control. If this is something you do, try asking yourself these questions:

- How is this logically my fault?
- Is there any way to prove that I'm wrong?
- What objective evidence supports this belief?
- What could I do to stop this from happening in the future?
- Was I actually in control of this situation?
- Am I being fair in my analysis of the situation?

Please don't forget that affirmations are not to be conflated with delusion. They shouldn't be seen as a way of making you think something wildly unrealistic is true. As weird as it sounds, we can influence how we respond to things, but we can't fully change how they might make us feel. This practice is meant to teach us how to better care for our minds, boost our self-esteem and shift our perspective. The reason this isn't the first thing I taught you is because I wanted to give you time to learn yourself properly so you're able to create an effective affirmation.

Using stock-standard mantras that don't resonate with you can backfire and leave you in a mental position far worse than when you began. Studies show that people who recite affirmations they don't believe, or that aren't applicable to their situation, can be left feeling worse than when they started.

Use positive language in conjunction with powerful body language for a more potent result. Social psychologist Amy Cuddy said that power posing (I've always thought this was standing upright, legs spread, arms in the air, but it can be any pose that makes you feel powerful) can actually boost your confidence levels.

If you're not seeing results, try switching up your language. Saying 'I will' rather than 'I am' can encourage realistic improvement at a pace you're more comfortable with.

THE PATH

TO

SUCCESS

* *Failures*

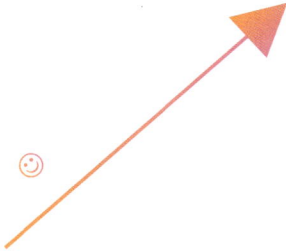

What people think the path to success is like.

What successful people know the path is like.

This is the part where I show you this drawing and remind you of the wobbly path to success. You don't want to see it as much I don't want to show it, but it's a necessary reminder. If the steps and chapters we've covered so far haven't felt as clear or concise as you'd imagined, that's because success isn't a linear journey. To convince you otherwise would be negligent.

I figured success out in retrospect. I think a lot of my career development to date has been because I didn't have any clear direction from the outset. This may sound nonsensical, so let's try visualising what I mean.

Imagine you're outside in the pitch-black (an analogy for a new or unknown experience, in case I've already lost you). Who knows how you got there, I sure don't, but I have it on good authority that you're not scared. You might not feel secure and you definitely don't have all the answers, but you're feeling comfortable enough to stay. You look left, right and behind you, but all you can see is a deep, dark abyss. However, when you swing back to the front you see a faint light in the distance and start to walk closer. As you do, you notice a paved concrete path illuminated by the light. Everything indicates that moving toward the light is the safest place to be, right? So, you move forward, barrelling into the brightness, looking straight ahead and paying very little attention to what you're walking on. DRAMA ALERT, chaos ensues! You end up stacking it and fall headfirst into the rubble.

You crack your phone screen and ruin your front and back camera, so now you can't even immortalise this incident virtually. When you look around properly, it turns out the footpath was under construction, but you were paying too much attention to the light at the end to notice. Now you're feeling unsafe, shaken up and a little bit resistant to picking yourself up to keep going.

In many ways this is how I perceive straight-line success. On this path, we become so sure that we're heading in the right direction that we don't mentally or physically prepare for any alternatives. So, when we fall down, it's a metaphorical kick in the shin, making it that much harder to get back up.

Now, let's put a hypothetical version of me into our original scenario and I'll demonstrate how I view the actual journey to success. While you noticed the light in the distance, I decided to plop down on the nearest bench and hang out on my phone. Not because I was smarter than you, had intel about the construction or wasn't drawn in by the light, but because I was comfortable with the idea of taking my time getting to my destination. Hours go by and I'm still lost on my phone (standard for me when I fall down a rabbit hole on the world wide web). The sun comes up and I can see that I'm in a park. Rather than following the paved concrete path, I notice something else in the distance and walk through the grass to suss out the opportunity.

These scenarios are a roundabout way of explaining to you that it's difficult to know which trajectory will lead you to the place you actually want to be, especially if you blindly tumble down the first path that appears. There is always more to know, more to learn and more to do. **Experience can prepare us for these situations, even if the journey to the destination isn't exactly what we had imagined.**

Life can be linear for heaps of people. You're a baby, a toddler, a child in primary school, a teen in high school, then a young adult and that's where life starts to peel into multiple directions. Perhaps you go to university and get a degree, then find a job in your field and work for forty years before you retire. Or you don't go to uni at all, but instead go straight to work, meet someone and start a family. Those two directions account for a significant portion of the population. I'd even go so far as to say that they are the norm.

If you don't follow that trajectory you can end up in a grey area. Where can I go? Who can I be? What can I do? We assume that when we eventually decide what it is we want to do that achieving our goals will be a straightforward process — this is how we've been conditioned to see progression. TV says go to uni and you'll get a job — reality says wrong. Magazines say eat celery and drink thirty-five litres of water and you'll attract the one — reality says lol, no. Radio says work hard and you'll have enough money to buy a home — reality says not quite, hon.

Maybe you're like me, someone who attempted a conventional career path. High school, uni (a two-time dropout) and then back to work in a few different offices in PR, social media management and digital marketing. Feeling unfulfilled, I quit that and became a DJ turned TV-presenter turned influencer, podcaster and now author. Anything but linear ... I couldn't really have planned for the winding path my career has taken. Even if I had made plans, there were so many things I couldn't have anticipated, like transitioning into a freelancer, making money off my personality, running a business and the complexity of explaining to people what it is I actually do.

Once upon a time when I was a teenager, I assumed that as an adult I would have a consistent and focused approach to my career because I was convinced that clarity, conviction and laser-beam focus just came with age. When that consistency wasn't working for me, all of my job changes began to feel like setbacks — albeit, exciting ones — until I read a vague statistic that told me most millennials will change their career (not job, career) between five and seven times in their life. This was both unbelievable and incredibly helpful for my self-esteem. Now I didn't feel like a failure; instead, I had proof that I was just a standard millennial.

If you think that this experiment will be the key to unlocking everything you've ever wanted, you have to realise that once you unlock your dreams there's more to attain and more to maintain. When I was a DJ, I assumed that playing music would be the extent of the job, the be-all and end-all. Nope, apparently it was just the first chapter. After a few months people started asking me when I'd make my own music, when I'd start my own radio show, if I could record my gigs and start vlogging cool parties I'd played at, when I'd start promoting my own events and if I'd be open to teaching people how to DJ. These requests opened up a floodgate of ideas in my mind and, naturally, being the action-oriented person I am, I started obsessing about scaling up and I asked myself what it would look like if I gave some of these suggestions a shot.

Sometimes it can feel like there is always something or someone telling you to strive for more, and even if you're not action-orientated it's hard to not be affected by these kinds of outside influences. For so long the idea of having more has been synonymous with 'betterness'. **While sometimes having more can be a great thing, that's not necessarily always the truth.** We have to remember that having more can also be excessive and gluttonous.

I'm not saying this to berate you for wanting more or to challenge you to want less, but let's have a think about what's influencing you either way. There are countless things to consider: the media, consumer culture, capitalism, comparison culture and, of course, how we've been conditioned to view success. But I could never know how these factors impact you on an individual level. Often we're driven to act through external motivations and other times those motivators are internal. What I do know is that in my time I've come across a few concepts that really put my relationship with consumption in perspective, and **the biggest thing I've learned is that you need to have an understanding of why you want more.**

THE DIDEROT EFFECT

Have you ever thought you'd be happy if you just bought that one thing, but when you buy it you realise there's yet another one thing you need and then another and another and another until you've gobbled up all your disposable income? The Diderot effect is a phenomenon coined by eighteenth-century philosopher Denis Diderot, who said 'The introduction of a new possession into a consumer's existence will often result in a process of spiralling consumption.' This basically means that when you buy one thing, your desire to buy more increases.

You want to treat yourself to a holiday, so you buy plane tickets. But now you 'need' a new swimming costume, sunglasses, camera and suitcase. The reality is, you'd have been fine if you'd just stuck to your initial purchase, however the act of buying the first thing propels you into a buying-cycle. There's no guide on how to stop this process, but I want you to think about how this effect works in relation to success. A lot of us have a thirst for one huge milestone that we think is going to be the solution to our problems. We work towards it, break our backs and lose sleep because we've convinced ourselves that the result is going to make everything worth it and we'll never need anything this badly again. Then you get what you want and realise the feeling of wanting doesn't ever really go away, and the cycle repeats. It's honestly an unavoidable process for the average person, which makes the challenge recognising the cycle and being more aware of whether your wanting something is from a place of lack (scarcity) or drive (abundance).

HUMAN INSTINCT

We see this cycle of wanting in our basic human instinct as well. Some researchers (in particular, neuroscientist Jaak Panksepp) say that there are seven main instincts in the human brain that impact the way humans behave. There's anger, fear, panic/grief, maternal care, pleasure/lust, play and seeking (which is apparently the most important). All mammals have the urge to seek, as they get a spike of dopamine when they discover new information, especially when it pertains to survival or general self-betterment. Because of this natural impulse, we presume that whatever we're yearning for will feel this void, when in reality we just like the feeling of discovering something new.

At one point, being a working DJ felt like I'd reached my goal and acquired success, but all the external feedback and new ideas and suggestions had my mind mashed up. All these different options felt like a million alternate paths to a new goal, and I didn't know what the end result would look like. I started getting frustrated. Why was I so fascinated by the idea of a more intense job? Why couldn't I just be content with what I had? Despite my frustrations, I tried some of the things others had suggested. I did some poorly and some well — but it didn't take long for these new directions to become a hassle.

The opportunity to be an MTV presenter took my mind off thinking about whether or not I'd achieved success in the music industry. If you hadn't noticed already, it's very on-brand for me to start things and not finish them. That's including, but not limited to, thoughts, ideas, projects, careers, relationships and food.

Even if the quest to get to where you want seems clear to you, there are still nuances to how you execute your plan. What I mean is that the journey from who we are to who we want to be isn't going to be straightforward, binary or one-dimensional. It's not from A to B or here to there. It's a series of events that are ever-changing and evolving, and I don't really think there is an end to that journey.

This experiment can be the key to unlocking everything you've always wanted to achieve. I believe that once you commit to the lifelong marriage of developing yourself, a number of things can happen and these experiences can be both positive and negative:

The commitment takes the pressure off knowing that the work never stops. If there is no immediate destination, then you have all the time in the world to get where you're going.

A life-long journey can feel like being in solitary confinement without committing a crime, trapped by the idea of wanting something you can't have right away.

Knowing that it could take you a lifetime to achieve your goals can slow down your motivation in the same way that knowing you have a finite time to achieve what you want can increase your motivation.

It might not affect how you work at all.

It might mentally paralyse you and repel you from trying.

I'm not saying this to deter you from trying or to bombard you with reasons to act, I just want to give you information. These things are all part of the human experience and knowing this should hopefully make your journey a little bit more digestible.

DON'T BE DUMB!

This is really an aggressive way of saying, try to consume more information! I used the word 'dumb' precisely because of the connotation it has. 'Dumb' is an insult that most of us have been dodging since primary school. No one wants to be perceived as dumb, but instead of learning and educating ourselves as a means to avoid this title, many of us will feign intelligence and self-awareness because it feels easier. Or, we'll commit to learning but cap ourselves at a certain level because you think you're the smartest person you know. After all, it can feel useless to keep absorbing information when the people around you aren't doing the same.

Have you heard of the quote, 'If you're the smartest person in the room, you're in the wrong room?' It's easy to disregard this as a cliché, but if you take a moment to dissect it, you'll see it's genius. How is it possible that you've managed to trump the intelligence of the majority of people you hang out with and why are you comfortable with that?

Enter a new room, please. For the sake of your perspective. It's easy to stick with what you know (why do you think in the last ten years I have only learned to make pasta and schnitzel?) and it can be comfy to latch on to people who aren't the brightest bulbs, but what's the point in that? It's like hanging out with pre-teens and feeling gassed when your vocab is too advanced for them. Of course, you're technically smarter than them, but you're still the same old, outdated version of you. In the nicest way possible ...

If your last bit of proactive learning was in high school or your first year of uni, then it is time to hit the books. **Your brain isn't a muscle, but make no mistake, it needs to be trained to keep it healthy and functioning.** No one is asking you to be the second Einstein, learn complex scientific theories or explain why deja vu happens; I'm simply advising you to commit to increasing your intelligence. Don't freak out, start small and begin to get more comfortable with researching and retaining information. If you're confused about where to begin, take little steps and work on tasks that you can execute easily. You know, googleable stuff — you have a phone and I'm making a bet that you have internet access. This ultimately means that you have an abundance of opportunities to soak in some new info.

I have a theory that the reason a lot of people don't proactively learn is because we've never really had to. Hear me out: when you're a child and a teenager, you're literally forced to go to an institution for nine months of the year to learn. Even if you didn't feel like it or want to, it was mandatory. In these learning spaces you didn't really have to apply yourself, be autonomous or even try because there was a teacher or lecturer dedicated to increasing your knowledge; their livelihood literally depended on it. Because this method of learning is so common, we're programmed to expect that we'll just know stuff through existing. We start to believe that understanding new words, concepts, theories and ideas will come to us and, if not, someone will teach us, right? Wrong. **So many of us haven't realised that we are no longer in environments that force intelligence on us; even fewer of us actually recognise that's how it was.**

So, when you get to adulthood you start to regard those who 'know things' as rare overachievers or the exception to the rule, you're not seeing that if you want to get smart (be less dumb!) then you actually have to do it yourself. You have to try! Most people will get by fine not applying themselves, relying on the data they have from just existing, but you strike me as someone different. Someone who's interested but doesn't know where to start. Someone who needs a bit of a push, so here it is. I challenge you to try to learn something every week, not because I guarantee that what you find out could be the key to your success, but because you need to be mentally prepped and primed to retain data. Not every activity you do is going to result in a prize, but it's still worth the effort. Here are some tips to get you started:

Learn a new word.

Research and trial new ways to resolve conflict.

Find out the cost of living in Norway and compare it to your country.

Read an article on something that you didn't know about.

Research what social customs are like in the Gambia.

When you're comfortable with that entry level dive-in, it's time to start researching psychological theories that affect you as a person. As I've reiterated a hundred different times before, a huge determining factor between you getting what you want (and what you don't want) is you. The external factors that impact most people (capitalism, patriarchy, socio-economic status, etc.) will obviously take a toll on you, but the damage can multiply when those factors collide with personal weaknesses.

You could have been raised in a single-parent, working-class home, which meant that you might not have had as many opportunities as those in your age group who came from two-parent, middle-class families. This could be due to income disparity, the limited presence of a parent or general insecurities that could come with not fitting 'the norm'. You might argue that this alone puts you at a disadvantage for certain career opportunities; but what if, in addition to this, you hadn't realised you have terrible time-management skills, poor attention to detail and a disdain for authority. While these things might not register as issues to you, we can argue that these internal points could have a worse impact than the external factors of your upbringing.

This is where introspection and evaluation come into play. Learning about yourself — the depths, the motivators and the triggers — doesn't just magically happen. Yes, you might be one of the lucky few who have an epiphany, but for the most part you either get forced into the realisation through a life-changing event (transitioning from teen to adult, breakups, getting fired or growing apart from friends) or you have to search. It's hard and, ultimately, never-ending because it's difficult to know what you're looking for to begin with, but when you find it, you're often changed for the better. **The sooner you realise how to mitigate the ramifications of the 'bad' traits you uncover, the more time you can spend leveraging the 'good'.** You've hacked the mainframe!

There are a few key psychological theories I came across during my self-development research that I think would really benefit you to learn. Each one helped to unlock a deeper grasp on myself and gave me tips on how to do it all better. Basically, these theories showed me all the ways I didn't know myself and how I could improve that immediately.

Self-serving bias — this concept details how our brain can struggle to assess scenarios objectively, preferring to blame external forces for the negatives, but to thank ourselves when good things happen.

Cognitive bias — a theory that highlights all the ways our brains are hardwired into subjective thinking.

The paradox of choice — the concept that when we're making decisions, having more options can make it harder to choose, causing more stress.

Decision fatigue — the idea that long periods of decision-making affect the quality of your choices.

It's ambitious to attempt to dissect yourself from scratch using only the information you already have, but there's an easier way. Experts and psychologists (like Sigmund Freud, Carl Jung, Leon Festinger, Carl Rogers and many more) have invested their lives in creating tools to help you understand yourself better. Take advantage of that resource and use this as your next challenge to be less dumb!

FOUR WAYS

TO IMPROVE

YOUR

PERSPECTIVE

1. *Be more* intentional. Try your hardest to be more self-aware. Not only do you need to be aware of what you're doing and why, but decide what you're going to do before you do it. Being intentional acts like a cognitive coping-mechanism, which helps you to focus and redirect your output.

2. *Get uncomfortable.* The definition of insanity is doing the same thing over and over and expecting a different result, so why don't you leap out of your comfort zone and try something new for a change? Take a different route home, research a topic that usually wouldn't interest you, try a new food or engage in a conversation that challenges you.

3. *Embrace troubleshooting.* It's OK to be wrong. It's OK not to understand. It's OK to make mistakes. It's how you recover from these setbacks (and how long it takes you) that's important. There once was a time where complaining about your problems felt like an effective method of troubleshooting: maybe if you nag enough, cosmic powers will swoop in and fix the issue, right? But why wait for the issue to maybe go away when instead you could learn to build your own resilience? The next time you're met with conflict, try a different method of resolution. Pessimists see problems where optimists see opportunities; try to see silver linings, gratitude and opportunities for growth.

4. *Dodge enemies* of progress. Positivity is contagious and pessimism is always looking for a best mate. Simply put, if you're having trouble maintaining an optimistic attitude then you need to scurry far away from energy vampires. You know who I mean, those people who suck all hope and life out of you with their presence alone. The people who counter your good news with bad and revel in any drama. It's fun, but it can be draining and damaging if you struggle to protect your space. Invest your time into people who help you grow and evolve.

WHAT'S A REACTION?

A reaction is typically quick, flippant, emotion-filled, tense and (passive) aggressive. Often our reactions will provoke a new reaction from the people we're interacting with. A reaction isn't result-oriented; instead, it can perpetuate anger and be unproductive. When we react, we're prioritising getting our point across — usually at the cost of creating a win–lose dynamic — rather than troubleshooting and working towards a resolution that suits all parties.

WHAT'S A RESPONSE?

A response is typically more chill, measured, nuanced and not dismissive of others. Responses invite the other party to engage in a healthy discussion that will often lead to understanding or a resolution. Responding allows you to be assertive without indulging in the superiority complex of a reaction. **To respond rather than react requires you to take your time and think of an outcome that best accommodates all parties.**

DECISION FATIGUE

PARADOX OF CHOICE COGNITIVE BIAS

CATASTROPHISING

CATASTROPHISING

COGNITIVE BIAS

DECISION FATIGUE

CONFIRMATION BIAS

SELF-SERVING BIAS

PARADOX OF CHOICE

PERSPECTIVE EXERCISE

Below are three intentionally vague scenarios I've constructed to demonstrate how a pessimist would handle a situation compared to an optimist. This exercise is to help you better understand how perspective can drastically change your outlook on experiences. I would like you to theorise how the situation could be navigated using two different perspectives: positive (abundance) and negative (scarcity).

I've been waiting months for a long weekend so I could take a low-key vacation to New Zealand, and now I've woken up late and missed my flight.

The pessimist says: 'Oh my God, of course this would happen to me! I'm a beacon for drama, what else can I expect? I'm so annoyed at myself! I feel so dumb and I can't even stand to deal with airport customer service because they're going to be useless. I just should cancel the whole trip and stay home.'

The optimist says: 'That's really frustrating. Now I know that I definitely need an alarm to wake up and should probably give myself more time to get ready for the airport. This isn't ideal, but I'll call airport customer service straight away and see what can be done. I'm sure they'll be able to help me deal with this and I'll be on a new flight in no time.'

Using my examples above as reference, it's clear how perspective can help you effectively troubleshoot a bad situation and move on with as little damage as possible. A slight change in language can heavily influence your emotional reflex and help you to respond instead of react. Here are two more hypothetical situations for you to practise on:

*My boss called me in for a performance review.
I was feeling really confident because they spent the first
thirty-minutes validating my work, but then told me they
won't be offering me a promotion.*

*I've been single for three years and have had pretty
average dating experiences. I recently met a person who
I get along with and we'd been seeing each other for four
months. I asked for us to be exclusive and they declined and
said they'd prefer to just be friends.*

By this point, I'm sure you can think of scenarios where you've reacted and not responded. Now is not the time to berate yourself; this is where we focus on moving onwards and upwards. The reason I'm encouraging you to learn these tools for self-mediation is because having the perspective required to **see hardship and difficulties as learning experiences is a fundamental building block to creating a successful and fulfilling life.**

As you work towards achieving more (money, experiences, pleasure, leisure or knowledge) the frequency of good outcomes increases just as much as the bad. As your success increases so too does your potential for failure. So, if you catch your internal dialogue acting childish, remember this exercise and keep training your brain to be resilient by thinking optimistically and abundantly.

Meet your subconscious mind

Did you know that your brain is constantly processing information? As you read these words your brain is still acutely aware of your environment and is storing everything. You are the USB cable and your brain is the hard drive.

Your conscious mind contains all the things you are currently aware of, like the smell of food wafting in from the restaurant next door, the space you're in, the words you're reading, your memories, feelings and fantasies. Every thought you recognise racing through your head is part of your conscious mind. Naturally, these thoughts have a huge effect on every single thing you do, think, say and experience.

Your subconscious mind contains all the things your conscious mind wants to hide from you. I'm not just over-dramatising, this is a theory that was studied and affirmed by popular psychologist Sigmund Freud. All those thoughts, urges, needs, wants and emotions that you don't even know you have live within your subconscious mind, and its job is simply to store and retrieve data. Your subconscious mind has virtually unlimited space and permanently stores everything that has ever and will ever happen to you. It's said that **our subconscious memory is perfect, but it's our ability to consciously recall data that's whack.**

The subconscious mind is a remarkable part of our brains, and while we're unaware of what it's doing and therefore not able to control it, scientists still believe it pretty much drives our behaviour.

Earl Nightingale, an author who writes about human character development, motivation, and how to cultivate a meaningful existence, says 'Whatever we plant in our subconscious mind and nourish with repetition and emotion will one day become a reality.' Tony Fahkry, a personal growth and self-empowerment expert, says that tasks which generally fall into the logical and analytical categories are performed via the conscious mind. Meanwhile, most actions and behaviours are believed to be governed by the subconscious mind, which is said to be 'irrational' compared to the controlled conscious mind.

As we discussed earlier, improving your perspective, reciting affirmations and being optimistic isn't a game you play to trick your brain into treating you better. It's not a reactive, one-time thing used to reverse any 'bad luck' you've gotten from being harsh on yourself. It's not a bit of feel-good delusion for a spike in dopamine. All the times you talked down to, bullied or reprimanded yourself have been captured indefinitely in your subconscious mind, and we're not in charge of how this will impact us in the future. Your brain doesn't know when you were just having a laugh or when you really meant it. With that in mind, it's important that we become really aware of what we're consciously teaching our brain. It's a lifelong process made miles easier simply by utilising more positive thinking and language.

WHAT'S SO SPECIAL ABOUT YOUR SUBCONSCIOUS MIND?

Your subconscious mind processes data based on what your conscious mind tells it, working tirelessly and thanklessly to make sure your behaviour fits a pattern consistent with your past actions and experiences. This means that when you think or do something repeatedly your subconscious will latch onto this information, presuming that it's important, and act in line with that behaviour.

Your subconscious mind doesn't think independently, it doesn't have an agenda and it doesn't learn anything unless you program it.

Let's say you consciously tell yourself that you're dumb, unworthy, impatient and lazy. You might not believe all these things about yourself, but you run these thoughts through your brain on the daily, regardless. You might even use them as excuses or justifications for your behaviour. When you're done actively thinking these negative things, your subconscious mind (aka your partner in crime) has noticed that pattern in your thoughts. It doesn't want you to work too hard, so it's going to take over from here and get the wheels of self-deprecation going on a continuous cycle. While you're asleep your subby mind is working overtime for you. Suddenly the negative thoughts you told yourself that were only temporary become part of your subconscious narrative, and you begin to believe all of those subjectively terrible things about yourself.

The thing is, your thoughts aren't the only thing that impacts your subconscious mind. It can be programmed by your environment, the media you consume and the people you speak to. We can't control what our subconscious mind latches on to. Have you ever wondered why you think the way you do? Why the colour red reminds you of passion or why you're scared of the dark (just me)? At some point in your life you've been explicitly or implicitly taught things, and though you may not have been aware of it, your brain was. Any limiting beliefs, fears, phobias, thoughts or ideas were taught to you at one point by an experience you had. This can be referred to as 'programming' or 'conditioning'.

It's dangerous to give you the impression that all your subconscious conditioning is inherently negative. I've no doubt there's a lifetime of good stuff in there, too. It's probably the reason why you say please and thank you, treat animals well, trust your peers and are open to talking to strangers.

You're probably thinking, OK, so how do I hack my brain and reprogram my subconscious? Well, it's really not that straightforward, and to be fair I don't have all the answers. If your subconscious mind operates away from your level of consciousness, then how are you actually supposed to change any of it? How are you supposed to be aware of the things that you theoretically aren't even aware of?

First, you need to **stop living life on autopilot, and start processing everything you feel, think and do.** Develop your own bespoke encyclopaedia of you. Make the mental switch from believing I am this way just because to realising I am who I am because of specific circumstances that I'll work to understand. You'll start to learn and trust that you know who you are, why you're this way, and in turn, what you want and why you want it. When this happens, you'll become more tapped into the moments where your brain is telling you to behave in ways that contradict what you 'know' you should do. Perhaps you're a chronic procrastinator who's working to reform themselves? However, when it's time to focus, your brain is telling you that it's the perfect moment to do anything but the task at hand. Don't be alarmed, it's just doing what you've subconsciously programmed it to from years of dillydallying and stalling tactics. **When you rebel against what feels like your intuition or base nature, and instead choose to consciously trust that what you think and the new decisions you make are right for you, it's then that you can truly manipulate your subconscious mind.**

NOW THIS IS WHERE IT GETS WILD!

I'm about to throw around some big words, so don't fall asleep on me — this information is vital. Your subconscious mind has this thing called a homeostatic impulse. Sound it out, it's phonetic. This impulse finds and mimics your body's mental, cognitive and physics patterns so you don't have to actively do them. To this end, the process of homeostasis is what regulates your body temperature, heartbeat and keeps you breathing regularly. Similarly, homeostasis works its magic in your mind and keeps you thinking and acting in a manner that's consistent with what you have done and said in the past. This is how your comfort zones and default behaviours are created.

When you act in a way that contradicts your normal patterns of behaviour, your subconscious mind reacts and tries to pull you back in line. Naturally, if it notices you acting whack, your mind presumes this is unintentional behaviour, perhaps a system error, and will attempt to force the pattern back into flow.

As a means to regulate this abnormal behaviour, your subconscious mind may send you an emotional reaction like tension or uneasiness. Sound familiar? **Your subconscious mind is the gatekeeper of your comfort zone, the friend zone for self-development, which is programmed full of unhealthy coping mechanisms.** These unhealthy coping mechanisms are why the greats are always telling you to push yourself out of your comfort zone!

In order to bulldoze your way out of the comfort zone, you have to be willing to conquer that uncomfortable or awkward feeling that comes when you try new things.

Learn how to recognise the low-level thoughts that pull you back down into a space of comfortable mediocrity.

Regularly check in with yourself. Take out the trash in your brain. Analyse how much time you actually spend on thoughts that aren't positive, realistic or conducive to growth. How much time do you spend berating yourself for things that aren't inherently your fault?

How much time do you spend wishing you were somebody else or praying that you'll magically acquire a new skill?

This way of thinking can do a lot of long-term damage to your mental health, and it's in your best interest to make sure that you are actively trying to combat that negativity.

Stop normalising negative thoughts. By making a conscious effort to focus on the positive, you'll eventually break down the negative thought-patterns you've developed and start to build a new pattern, which allows you to reach a higher level of competence.

Section Two

STEP THREE

Chapter Three:
Know What You Want

STEP FOUR

Chapter Four:
Know Why You Want It

STEP THREE

Know
you

CHAPTER THREE

what
want

WHAT THIS CHAPTER *WILL* TEACH YOU

Why intention matters when it comes to setting goals

Why your goal needs an aim and then a plan

Why figuring out what you'd lose sleep over is integral

The difference between realistic and unrealistic goals (and why they're both important)

The difference between short- and long-term goals, and how to set them

What your bad habits can teach you about motivation, commitment and goal setting

The difference between what you want now versus what Future You wants

THREE

Why it's important to have determination and resolve

That a lack of passion isn't your problem

WHAT THIS CHAPTER *WON'T* TEACH YOU

How to bullshit yourself into wanting things you don't need

How to waste your time

In the last few chapters I explained that before I can give you the tools to get what you want, I need you to know who you are and who you want to be. As you've learned, your thoughts, motivations, strengths, weaknesses, barriers and fears will impact the journey to getting what you want. You're a unique individual so it only makes sense that the path you take is bespoke; personalised just for you. Now you've done enough deep thinking and self-evaluation to graduate to the next step.

What do you want?

Keeping in mind everything you've learned about yourself thus far.

What
Do
You
Want?

I'm hoping that all the work you've done up until this point has given you a clear idea on what you want, because I can't tell you. That was never part of the experiment.

It's a tough question to answer in any context. What do you want to eat? What do you want to be when you grow up? What do you want to wear at your funeral? It always feels so loaded. Is it because most of us aren't lucky enough to get what we want? Maybe we're just used to settling, rather than advocating for ourselves because we're scared of being let down? Or perhaps we simply have so little trust in the process that we'd prefer to pretend that we don't have a preference; we say things like, 'I haven't really thought about it,' or 'I'm not fussed,' when in reality we're anything but indifferent.

I want you to get into the mindset that you can have anything within reason. I don't want you to fake it till you make it, I want you to actually believe that you can have the Thing you want. I grew up with a mum who instilled a hectic amount of confidence in me, one who believed in me so much that it felt ridiculous to not see the potential she saw. If you don't have the luxury of being raised by my mum it doesn't mean you're doomed; you just need to take the time to figure out how you build your own sense of self-confidence.

As clichéd as it may sound, a good way to get a clearer idea of what you want is to picture exactly what it would look, feel and sound like if you had it:

Where are you?

Do you feel safe?

Does this feel right?

What can you see?

What emotions are you experiencing?

How would you describe this to someone else?

Having to really imagine what achieving your goal would be like means you're taking extra time to consider what you want and how it can manifest into reality. And yes, although it's a cliché, I do think it's helpful to ask yourself this question: If you didn't have to work, if you didn't have any responsibilities, if your only vocation in life was to do whatever you want, what would you actually do? Not because this is something to aspire to (we live in the real world where it's beneficial to have more practical desires), but because this might highlight areas of importance that you haven't thought about at length before.

Personally, I find a lot of joy in psychology, anthropology, sociology and consulting with people. I love understanding why people are the way they are and how that inherently affects the way they behave. I love to quiz people to try to better understand them and activate my objective brain when I try to assist them. I love analysing their situations and giving them advice, but not actually being liable for the choices they make. All this means I spend a lot of time daydreaming about random situations I've overheard or read and thinking about what kind of guidance I would give. That's just because I'm nosy and think I'm smart, but these interests have also been helpful in unlocking my own biases and blind spots. It's taught me how I'm able to use a rational and logical mind when analysing someone else's situation, but can easily revert to being a bit of a baby when it comes to my own.

For me, all of those factors have been important cornerstones of my personal goal-setting. My aim is to incorporate my passions into my overarching plan.

I do this because I know that if I can integrate what I love with what I have the bandwidth to actually do, I'm going to be happy.

I'm aware that not everyone else has found their life-affirming thing just yet, and that's why I'm here. I can't tell you what yours is — nobody but you can do that — but helping people understand themselves and what they want to do is something that brings me joy and purpose. So, I'm going to steer you in the right direction with the next activity.

WHAT WOULD YOU LOSE SLEEP OVER?

1. *Is a* good night's sleep important to you? Why?

2. *What have* you happily lost sleep over in the last three months and why?

3. *What have* you unhappily lost sleep over and why?

4. *Can you* avoid losing sleep to negative experiences in the future? How would you do this?

5. *What would* you choose to lose sleep over in the next three months, and why?

Now it's time to analyse your answers and see if there are any key themes that come through. The reason I centred the activity around losing sleep is because we all know that a solid sleep is crucial for good health, and prioritising tasks that aren't time-sensitive over your eight hours of bliss says more than you think.

Anyone could tell you that you're more likely to succeed when your career goals are specific. So, start by peering into the future and create a vision for your ideal self and career. What would that look like in one, three, or five years? What about the next decade, or the one after that? What does your ideal life look like? What is Future You doing and what does fulfillment and success look like for them? The answers to these questions provide a good framework to strategise backwards from.

Self-belief is paramount to success.

LEGITIMATE GOAL SETTING:
Realistic versus unrealistic

The section is shady for a reason, and that's because not all goals are made the same. There is a time and place to delude yourself (New Year's resolutions; losing weight in winter to be snatched for summer; pretending you won't be cramming before a big test), but this chapter isn't it. We've now reached the point where we can talk about your legitimate goal.

Goal setting can be dangerous for people who suck at following through with their plans. Setting out goals tempts us to dream big — after all, that's the whole point — but it's also possible to dream too big for your own capabilities. Not because what you want is within the realm of impossibility, but because the strengths, skills and determination you have just aren't conducive to achieving what you want. This isn't the part where we blast 'Eye of the Tiger' and you tell me about that career fantasy you need the luck of a lotto winner to achieve. It's great to flex your imagination, but when we spend too much time thirsting for the improbable it can start to affect you negatively. Similar to what we've already covered in our discussion on affirmations, it's beneficial to say nice things to yourself if you believe them, but if you know you're just lying to yourself this can magnify feelings of inadequacy. **A better feeling is the warmth of an attainable win.**

We all have the propensity to get a little excited and wrapped up in the narrative of our future success, a feeling which can then drive us to make unrealistic (although sometimes motivating) goals. We can get so fixated on one idea of fortune, that anything else feels like a consolation prize, or worse, failure. When you do something you thought was almost impossible you get a kick of confidence which, if unchecked, can make you feel like you are invincible. Hubris that's not matched with skill and consistency will result in quick peaks and massive drops. And what's the impact of that? A crushing blow to a person's confidence and self-esteem, something which makes it hard to build resilience.

You're not guaranteed success just because you've had it in the past.

I see the value in both wanting things that are far removed from your immediate lifestyle and pining for what you could have tomorrow if you applied yourself today. Those two ways of thinking exist on opposite ends of the spectrum but can coexist healthily if you want them to. For the best results, I advocate supporting any dream with realistic goals that allow you to focus on achievable outcomes.

Realistic goals are not to be confused with easy goals. If you've just started uni and the first thing on your to-do list is to become the CEO of a million-dollar company within the year, you can park that goal under 'unrealistic'. Given the fact that you probably lack the time, experience, resources and business acumen, not because you're young. A different person would tell you to forget that dream completely, but I know that crazier things have happened. I mean, planes can fly, and boats can float, and there was a point in time when the concept of those things would've been laughable. Despite the absurdity of inventing anything innovative from scratch, there always needs to be a set of realistic and achievable goals to make such a bizarre idea work.

When dreaming big and reaching for the stars, it's important not to let our realism veer into self-stifling pessimism. It's all a balancing act. So, you may not be able to become a CEO in your first year of uni, but that's not an excuse to develop a limiting mindset.

I know exactly what I want, so what's the point in wasting my time doing anything but?
Well, it's not wasted time if you make it a learning opportunity. The person who sees that they don't have the range to accomplish one of their goals doesn't eliminate all future goals, they recalibrate. It's unlikely that you only want one thing, and fixating on something you don't have the resources to pursue, then self-sabotaging and choosing not to do anything at all in an act of defiance is extremely childish! Establish some new priorities. Start smaller, work your way towards your ultimate dream in incremental steps, segment your goals so that half are driven by reality and others are driven by fantasy.

In order to give yourself peace of mind and a fighting chance at the success you want on your own terms, you have to be in control of your mental dialogue. As we know, the brain can't tell the difference between reality and fantasy and your subconscious mind stores everything you ever consume. Now is the time to unlearn the negative self-talk, self-deprecation and the inaction that's rooted in fear. Give yourself a chance to succeed by feeding your mind with the good stuff. Critical thinking, introspection, positive self-talk and self-appreciation are the equivalent of vegetables for the brain. You need your regular dose for a healthy mind.

It takes a very sensible and self-aware person to say, 'I would love to own a business one day, but I'm not a leader and hate managing people, so while that might be an unrealistic goal I'll still write it down so I can acknowledge it as a want' or 'My dream is to start a new life overseas but due to a global pandemic that will have to be postponed.'

While being realistic with your goals is paramount, it's also important not to rule things out straight away; give the idea room to marinate and evolve. Park it for a few weeks, months or years. No one is saying that because you can't do what you want, when you want, that it should be crossed off your list indefinitely.

Your job is to set realistic frameworks around the things you want, to make sure that when you're in a position to pursue them, you can start with a clear enough vision. Let's use this example of owning a business to help you understand how to discern if a goal needs to be parked in unrealistic territory or re-evaluated to find the parts of it that are realistic. Break your goal down into pieces and allow yourself to get to the root of what you actually want.

Do you want the autonomy of working for yourself?

Do you want more money?

Do you like the flexibility of having more than one role?

Do you want more spare time?

Do you want to set your own deadlines?

Do you want to be the boss, set the standards and make the rules?

Do you want financial independence?

Ask yourself critical questions and be truthful about your answers because they will give you a deeper insight into whether or not you should go forth, full-speed ahead, or pivot and prioritise something else.

Realistic and unrealistic goals exist on a spectrum; goals don't need to be completely one or the other, they're subject to change based on your circumstance and approach.

Realistic goals should take into consideration the means you have right now — your time, money and skills — in addition to the means you know you're able to acquire easily. Unrealistic goals aren't contingent on immediate possibilities or reality, but they are still things that you yearn for. The kind of thing you'd probably avoid telling others about because they'd ask you to be more practical. These goals should not be forgotten. Keep them in mind to fuel your aspirations.

ADJUST YOUR
MINDSET.

ASSESS YOUR
OPTIONS.

PLAN!

HOW TO DISCERN BETWEEN REALISTIC AND UNREALISTIC GOALS

As we've discovered, your ability to achieve what you want is about so much more than the want itself. It's about who you are, the privilege you have, the resources you have access to, the time, money and energy you can commit to it and, of course, the logical steps you'll take to get there. The following activity will help you troubleshoot your realistic and unrealistic goals. Use these answers to develop an understanding of what you need to learn or explore before you can make these dreams a reality.

Write down three realistic goals you have.
   a. What makes these goals realistic for you?
   b. What is it about these goals that interests you?
   c. What behaviours or traits of yours will make it easier to achieve these goals?
   d. What skills will you have to learn to achieve this goal?

Write down three unrealistic goals you have.
   a. What is it about these goals that interests you?
   b. Why do you think these three goals are unrealistic?
   c. What behaviours or traits of yours make these goals difficult for you to achieve?
   d. What skills would you have to learn in order to achieve these goals?

TANGIBLE VS INTANGIBLE GOALS

Obviously, not all goals are made equal. Some are easy, some are hard; some are realistic, some are not; some take a few hours of unrelenting focus and others take years of dipping in and out. Regardless of the type of goal you're working towards, the more specific you are about your aims, the better. Get in the habit of knowing exactly what you want. What it looks like, feels like, how much energy it'll take and what skills you'll need to achieve it.

That being said, we need to get out of the habit of thinking that the goals we can't clearly articulate aren't important. I began the practice of separating my goals into tangible and intangible categories after realising that, more often than not, I was chasing a feeling or response that I couldn't quantify.

Sometimes there is an intersection between tangible and intangible goals, but it's only when we're able to mentally separate the two that we can identify what we actually want. Until we begin to segment and compartmentalise the types of goals we want, we're not going to be able to achieve them any time soon. Clarity is key! A few things to consider:

There is a difference between getting paid to create art and being recognised as an artist.

There is a difference between making a six-figure salary and being able to live luxuriously.

There is a difference between hiring your first employees and learning how to effectively lead a team.

There is a difference between getting an industry award and becoming an expert in your field.

There is a difference between getting a degree and being employable.

MY DISTINCTION BETWEEN SHORT- AND LONG-TERM GOALS

There are so many clichés which remind us that getting what we want isn't as simple as just wanting and immediately obtaining it:

Greatness doesn't happen overnight.

Good things come to those who wait.

A year from now you'll wish you'd started today.

While you could be the exception to the rule and randomly win the lotto or become an unlikely viral sensation overnight, for the most part, getting what you want takes time. As you continue to set and achieve your goals, you'll soon realise that the challenge isn't just how you're going to get it, but how not to lose momentum when achieving takes you longer than anticipated.

Waiting is not a concept I'm comfortable with. I hate waiting for responses to my emails, for my food to come once I've ordered it or packages to arrive in the mail. Just the thought of waiting makes me irritable. Yes, it's a bit entitled, but I'm blaming my feelings towards waiting on the fact we live in the age of convenience — it's connectedness on steroids. We can speak to anyone, anywhere instantly. Fashion, music, news, sport, therapy, entertainment, advice, love, relationships — they're all literally a swipe, tap or call away.

If you live in a metropolitan area, or have access to the world wide web, you know what it's like to get what you want as soon as you want it. Want to know the capital of Antarctica? Google it. Want waffle fries from a restaurant thirty minutes away? Order it. Want to know what species of plant is growing outside your house? There's an app for that.

I've consciously and subconsciously gotten so used to getting quick results that I have to remind myself it can't always happen that way. Remember this when you're setting goals and feeling disheartened or demotivated because you're not achieving them as fast as you'd anticipated.

With this in mind, I find it helpful to set goals that are time specific. Not as a way to guess how long it'll take me to reach them (and then bully myself when I don't), but so I can set a realistic framework on which goals to prioritise. If it's something you want and you have the means to accomplish it right now, then there's no reason it can't be considered a short-term goal. If you don't have the means, skill or time, and the goal is unrealistic or simply not a pressing concern, then it makes sense to push this back and make it a long-term goal.

SHORT-TERM GOALS

Time is relative, so it's up to you to deduce how short 'short' is for you, but my recommendation is to set your focus on a few days, weeks or months. These time frames are the entry-level, beginner-friendly tool to help anyone transform from 'someone who wants to succeed' to 'successful person'. They're powerful, underrated, and completely necessary. These short-term goals reflect the way most people see the world — immediate, instant, rewards-based and centred on gratification.

Short-term goals can act as relatable reminders of what you want to achieve, while the added time pressure gives you more motivation to get it done. Remember the cliché 'out of sight out of mind'? If you can't see what you need to do, it can be easy to forget that you want it; not because you don't care, but because life happens. While we're planning our big dreams we can fail to remember that we have daily priorities like work, school, socialising and hobbies.

Aside from the fact that it feels good to get things done, doing the less intense or time-sensitive stuff first can boost your morale and get you in the right headspace for your big goals. When your short-term goals are mapped out effectively, they can also act as mini milestones — a step-by-step guide that handholds you toward your long-term goals.

Long-term goals can be difficult, as they're set far enough away that it's easy to lose sight of them, and because of this, they are way harder to keep yourself accountable to. Telling yourself that your goal is to make one hundred thousand dollars annually through freelance work is completely different from setting a goal to update your website and portfolio.

Setting short-term goals can give you a clear insight into what your current capabilities are, providing you with a better understanding of what it takes to execute a long-term goal. Do you know how much time, money or energy you'd need to allocate to your long-term goal? If not, then a short-term goal of yours should be to find out.

As a highly competitive person who likes to succeed but struggles to manage her time, I thrive on that winning feeling. With this in mind, I like to prioritise my wants based on what's actually achievable — it's important for me to know that I have a dopamine hit incoming at all times. I do this by transforming banal and draining tasks into games that will render me the winner and reward me for my efforts. I would like to say this is a failsafe way to ensure I get everything done, but there are tons of other factors inhibiting me from doing the things I should.

Behavioural psychologists have been telling us for years that people respond positively to having their achievements recognised, no matter how small. When I was in primary school, I distinctly remember receiving a participation award. An award just for showing up; for nothing more than getting involved! So, while I bludged my way through PE or gossiped during Rock Eisteddfod, I was still celebrated and, as we've already established, I thrived on the constant positive reinforcement. Much to my chagrin, these juvenile motivational tools were not something that carried through to adulthood. Bosses don't congratulate you for showing up to work, and lecturers definitely don't pat you on the back for coming to class. While these participation awards didn't give me the push I needed to actually shut my yap and fully engage, they did instil a certain confidence in me. One that affirmed that even if I didn't try, I would be rewarded. All this told me was that if one day I wanted to give something my 145 per cent, the worst that could possibly happen would be that I'd be validated more.

While there's been tons of research debunking the long-term efficacy of making all children and teens feel like they're winners regardless of their varying skill-levels, as adults we should be able to use some of this practice to our benefit. We know that in this big, bad capitalist world, you won't be validated if you don't contribute something of perceived worth. However, **it's important that we configure our own compass of personal pride so that we have the ability to dictate when we believe we are worthy of praise.** This allows us to take responsibility and dedicate more time to giving ourselves props when necessary so we can build confidence and continue to succeed.

One of the greatest enemies of progress is poor self-esteem and a lack of confidence. If you don't believe you can do something, or worse, if you believe that the outcome of trying will always be failing, then you won't try. Building up our self-esteem through regular praise is crucial. The first step is to **get comfortable with validating yourself instead of waiting for others to do it for you.** The second is to recognise when we've done something that is deserving of praise; it doesn't need to be the most amazing thing ever, start with the small things that made you feel proud. Yay, you woke up! You got to work on time! You finished that book! You reached out to a friend! You sent that email! Learn to be grateful to yourself for doing the Thing, whatever that may be.

We're not self-celebrating as a means to develop a skewed and inflated sense of self, but so we learn the power of congratulating ourselves to build resilience. Our ability to bounce back after 'failing' should resemble a basketball, not a deflated stress ball. Regular and realistic recognition of your successes will keep your ball of self-esteem nice and full.

All that being said, it's also important that we don't delude ourselves and grow overconfident from all the little wins we stack up. Be careful not to let those small chores serve as a distraction from the bigger priorities.

Constantly overcoming minor tasks only gives us the tools to keep achieving in small increments, and these mini wins need to be done in tandem with other short-term tasks that have greater difficulty. Rewarding yourself for replying to emails the day you receive them only builds your proficiency in replying to emails, right?

Remember what you're working towards and create tasks based on that. Let's say your short-term goal is to learn something new every week, the aim of that being to give you a better idea of what you need to do to transition from full-time work to freelance. It's worth keeping in mind that not everything you do is applicable to your primary short-term goal. While I'm sure learning to curl your hair is great for client first impressions and I've no doubt that perfecting your two-ingredient pancake recipe is the perfect lunchtime snack, these are not on topic. To make sure you stay focused, create a framework of things you know will be helpful and then work towards researching them.

While you're building up your personal confidence it's important to remember that these wins have only been awarded based on your own perception of your efforts. These wins don't automatically translate to other people's experiences. For one person, a short-term goal could be saving one thousand dollars, and for others it might be hiring ten employees. It's all relative. Don't become victim to the comparison game and try to match your experiences to others. Whatever milestone you need to set to get to where you want to be is OK; even if it takes you longer than you thought it would, you feel defeated and overwhelmed or you take a break from your goal because it's not garnering results. Take whatever steps you need on your personal journey to success, always remembering to focus on building good habits, improving your mindset, tracking your progress, celebrating yourself and, of course, getting support and encouragement from your loved ones when you need it.

TYPES OF SHORT-TERM GOALS

The best practice for setting your own short-term goals it to make them achievable, attainable, clear and defined. What you want to do and how you plan to do it should be crystal clear.

Send three networking emails by five pm today.

Make a daily post to your Instagram business-page for a month.

Give your resume a tidy and facelift by the end of the week.

Consume thirty minutes of educational media every day.

Make a date in the calendar to see a friend.

Submit your tax return at least a week before the due date.

LONG-TERM GOALS

What will your life will be like in five, ten or even twenty years? Will you still be clocking eight hours of screen time a day? Has your obsession with fast fashion waned? Are you still in that job? Did you ever make it to Morocco for that vacation you've been dreaming of? Have you kept the same friends? Will you be living in the same apartment? Will you still want the same things you do now?

I take solace in the fact that life can get better, worse or stay the same — two of those are pretty good options for most. To improve the odds of living the lifestyle that matches our fantasies, it helps to set long-term goals. I'm warning you now that these goals are generally life-changing, intimidating and seemingly set in an alternate universe.

Thinking about how much effort, energy and focus you'll need to achieve your long-term goal can seem overwhelming, and this pressure can lead to inaction. Feeling stuck or like you're unable to make any noticeable progress is normal. When this happens to me, I prioritise my short-term goals or start seeking out my participation-award tasks to make my progression obvious (but also to make myself feel better).

Although big-picture goals can sometimes seem impossible to achieve, it doesn't mean we shouldn't try to work towards them. The point of trying is to get you closer to your prize and it's not always guaranteed that you'll actually get it. It's a hard pill to swallow, but the sooner you come to terms with the idea that you might not always achieve what you set out to do, the easier it is to manage your own expectations.

The trick is to not bog yourself down with huge, mountainous tasks that will take you eighty years to complete. Instead, set achievable goals. I encourage you to think about where you want to be and to break it down into a number of smaller short-term goals to keep you on track. I personally have very few specific long-term goals. I've convinced myself that despite what I think I'll want in the future, what I've achieved by going with the flow has been rewarding enough for me. I know the kind of effort it requires to stay on track in the long term, and I know that I'm too lazy for that. Instead, I allow myself complete leniency and focus on developing myself in a way that suits my needs and personality.

When I was twenty, I'd convinced myself that I wanted to work in PR after fangirling Kelly Cutrone when bingeing on The Hills. She was ballsy, bossy and she got shit done. Although she presumably worked hard, it seemed like she reaped heaps of benefits just by having staff who worked under her. A bunch of sweet, less ballsy but still very passionate women. They all seemed to live quite charmed lives, dressed well, travelled, had great relationships and loved their jobs. I found their experiences aspirational and achievable. So, like an octopus tentacle to a boat, I latched onto the idea and began my career in PR. I applied to a private college, which cost way too much money considering I dropped out before I graduated. I got an internship a few months into the course, then when the agency offered me a day of paid work, I jumped at the chance. I enjoyed my work in PR as much as was feasibly possible seeing as I was burnt-out, overworked and felt like I couldn't catch a break. There was so much I didn't know, which was to be expected because I was a junior, but I just wasn't comfortable with being a newbie. Making mistakes and not excelling made me feel insecure because, as you know, I tied my self-worth into my career output.

Despite all of my obvious hang-ups, I really thought I was going to stay in

PR forever. Not because I thought I was going to be an amazing publicist, run my own agency and win heaps of industry awards, but because I'd put all my eggs in the one basket and didn't anticipate the need to do something else. This was The Plan. Staying put and working my way up became a long-term goal. Getting to the point I was at felt so unexpected and rare that my gratitude kept me in place. At the time I felt self-conscious, but also really lucky. Who was I to think I could do anything better when there were people far more talented than me who were satisfied with this as their career choice? Even when I started DJing, it took a significant amount of revenue for me to understand that I was now making enough money to not have to work in PR anymore.

The point here is not to denounce long-term goals; they're obviously very effective in their own right. These goals direct our actions, provide us with a sense of purpose and they can even shape our attitude towards thoughts, people or our particular situation. That being said, I definitely understand some of the hesitation people have with setting long-term goals. It's easy to think, *I barely know what I want now*. How am I meant to know what I'm going to want in the future? Thoughts like this are valid, of course, and believe me when I say that most people relate. However, giving your goals guidelines and structure is supposed to make you feel less insecure about whether or not you can achieve them; your long-term goals are not meant to trap or limit you from considering any other options.

Current You is not meant to know exactly what Future You needs.

Current You is meant to create a life that Future You is grateful for. Current You is also meant to put in the work and do what's required so that you can be comfortable and content with your future. **Current You is building the foundation, learning the skills and improving their mindset so that Future You can operate at the optimum level.**

Every fulfilling journey begins with action; you just need to step in the right direction. Where do you want to go? Envision a day when you are at your best: What are you doing? Where are you? How do you make money? Who are you with? Look for the broad themes as well as the details of what this day looks like. This vision should excite and motivate you. It should give you the materials to make your goals a reality.

HOW TO ACTUALLY SET A SHORT- OR LONG-TERM GOAL

SMART is an acronym that stands for Specific, Measurable, Achievable, Relevant, and Timely. In an ideal world, you'll have a higher probability of achievement if you incorporate all of these factors into your goal.

SPECIFIC

The specifics of your goal should be particular, clearly defined and not ambiguous. The more specific you are, the easier it is to theorise exactly what needs to be done to complete your goal.

What do you want to achieve?

Do you require someone else to pull you up so you can get shit done?

What do you need to complete this goal and do you have access it?

Instead of creating a vague goal like 'I want to start an online clothing store', a more specific goal would be 'I want to apply for an ABN, write a business plan and buy a website domain so I can start my online clothing store.'

MEASURABLE

Your goals should have criteria with which you can measure how you're tracking.

What is your indicator of progress? Is it social media likes, number of units sold or resumes sent, or a specific amount of money earned?

How do you know when you've completed the goal?

'I want to apply for an ABN, write a business plan and buy a website domain so I can start my online clothing store. **Every week, I'll aim to check one of these things off the list until it's complete.'**

ACHIEVABLE

You need to be completely honest with yourself to determine if this is a realistic or unrealistic goal.

Can you achieve this with the resources and skills you currently have? If not, can you learn or obtain the resources and skills that you need?

Is this goal actually possible; do you know someone else who's done it before?

Are you going to see this through?

'I want to apply for an ABN, write a business plan and buy a website domain so I can start my online clothing store. Every week, I'll aim to check one of these things off the list until it's complete. I personally know plenty of people who have done it before, and there are tons of resources that make the process super beginner-friendly. If I have trouble, I know I have people I can ask for help.'

RELEVANT

Specific goals are often components of larger, long-term strategies. It's important to know whether the task you're doing is necessary or if it's just advanced procrastination. Ask yourself:

Does this task benefit me?

Is this task required to fulfil my overall goal?

Is this a worthwhile use of my time?

Is the effort I put in going to encourage the desired outcome?

Am I the right person to execute this goal?

'I want to apply for an ABN, write a business plan and buy a website domain so I can start my online clothing store. Every week, I'll aim to check one of these things off the list until it's complete. I personally know plenty of people who have done it before, and there are tons of resources that make the process super beginner-friendly. If I have trouble, I know I have people I can ask for help. I've spent a few years curating my clothing store business locally at markets, but I believe that in order to scale up and reach more customers I need to make a website.'

TIMELY

How quickly the tasks need to be achieved changes depending on whether they are short- or long-term goals. This means that dragging a short-term goal out for months isn't the most efficient idea. A clear timeline of your task from beginning to end can help create some urgency. Before you set your objective, figure out if you even have time for this goal. Every goal needs a deadline so you can activate your laser-focus and get it done.

Can I allocate the appropriate time for this goal?

How long will each individual task take?

Is there a deadline?

What can I do today to make a start?

'In the next three months, I want to apply for an ABN, write a business plan and buy a website domain so I can start my online clothing store. Every week, I'll aim to check one of these things off the list until it's complete. I personally know plenty of people who have done it before, and there are tons of resources that make the process super beginner-friendly. If I have trouble, I know I have people I can ask for help. I've spent a few years curating my clothing store business locally at markets, but I believe that in order to scale up and reach more customers I need to make a website. **I'm allocating myself one main task a week to ensure I keep the momentum up. This week I'm going to speak to my friends who are business owners to ask them for any advice.'**

EXTRA TIPS TO MAKE SURE YOUR GOALS DON'T REMAIN FANTASIES

Set goals around what you actually want, not goals that sound cool to talk about.

Achieve your goal and then move on to the next one. It's exciting to have heaps of projects going on at once, but this makes it easy to become scatterbrained.

Be consistent and accountable; do things when you say you will.

Know yourself, know your skills and know your capabilities.

DETERMINATION AND RESOLVE

To be determined is to be persistent and have a firm purpose. Determination is the result of making a firm decision and being resolved not to change it.

By this point in our experiment you should have a better idea of who you are, who you want to be and what you want from life, either personally or professionally. If you're not feeling one hundred per cent confident in any of those categories, that's OK. It's difficult to feel secure in your decision-making when you're learning new concepts. Don't feel bad or disheartened, it's a lot of information to process at once and I know what it feels like to focus so hard on the words that we forget to practically apply what we're learning.

If this is how you're feeling, I'm going to quickly direct you whence you came for guidance. My tip for you is to re-read everything up to this point, but with a slightly different lens. Take time to understand the theory of every concept, then try to apply it to yourself and your situation before you move onto the next. Review your previous answers for all the activities to see if you still feel the same or if your approach has evolved in any way. Prioritise the concepts that didn't click initially and take your time with them. If you can, discuss these ideas with someone else to see if there are areas where they can help you to understand better.

I'm all about being fluid, malleable and adaptable; those are invaluable traits, which will always be beneficial. BUT there comes a point where everyone needs to put on their steadfast hat and stick to it.

It is always subject to change. It can be anything from routine to skills, a person to a job, or in this instance, a goal. Up until this point you've had literally all the time in the world to um and ah about what it is that you want. **You've done so many activities to re-evaluate and enforce what your Thing is.** Now it's time to stick to your guns and see it through until you know you've tried your hardest. I've written this book with a career lens, showing you skills, theories and ideas that can help you build success in that arena. However, you can still use these concepts and apply them in a personal context too.

I can't really teach you determination and resolve if you don't want to learn. I can give you all the tips and tricks I know, but the fact is if you don't really want it you won't try hard enough to learn. If you're wondering why you keep making plans only to slip up, it's very likely that you might not want what you're trying to achieve as badly as you think you do. Don't look at me that way, I'm right and you know it! The fundamental truth is, if you really wanted it, you would've done it or at least attempted it. You would've researched, reached out to someone, applied what you've learned, strategically thought about it — anything.

Sometimes the hardest pill to swallow is the fact that sometimes you just don't want the things you think you do.

That's why so much of this book calls for you to dig deep and build your self-awareness to understand yourself properly. How you respond to information will impact whether you succeed or not; do you critically assess it? Do you ask more than one person so you can compare, cross-reference and evaluate? Do you try, draw conclusions from your results and then try again? The same data can be given to ten different people and result in ten different outcomes because their individual perspectives, perceptions and behaviours will influence how they respond to everything.

It's up to you to recognise who you really are and what you really want so that you're less influenced by the noise around you telling you who to be, what to think and where to go. It's time to focus on what you actually need to do to be comfortable with your life. To take accountability for the choices you make.

I'm not here to tell you that you can be whoever you want to be and do whatever you want, because that's not true and I don't want to set you up for failure.

> **There are so many limitations with striving for success, because humans are limited, contradictory people.**

We need to be comfortable but also need to be pushed out of our comfort zones. We seek familiarity but find ourselves bored by the same old thing. We build habits that are enjoyable, although not beneficial to us, and wonder why we haven't evolved into more well-rounded people. We forget that who we are has been influenced by the factors around us, like our upbringing, friends, society, the media and the internet; by not acknowledging these things we don't realise that they might be inhibiting our growth. How do we separate ourselves from what we actually want versus what we've been conditioned to want? We do it by building our self-awareness, upskilling, self-reflection and willingness to apply feedback.

Let me tell you about some of the vices I have in life. I eat too much junk food. I spend too much time watching trash TV and far too much money on depreciating items. If I'm super hungry at night and all my local restaurants are closed, I've been known to get a taxi to a fast-food place twenty minutes away. That's how desperate and determined I am to fill my body with preservative-based poison. Let's think about how many hours of my life I've spent streaming movies, TV shows and YouTube. Twenty hours a week, maybe forty? I'm asking friends for links. I'm paying for Netflix. I'm invested in the lives of people I don't know and will never meet. Some would regard this as just entertainment, necessary for an enriched life (which I won't dispute), but all these things can be regarded as me working time and time again, committing hours to fulfilling my goal of watching stuff online.

Now, here's the painful bit. If I had to think about all the goals of mine that I quit at the first thought of hardship I would be sent into a deep depressive state. If I thought about all the silly barriers that I'd interpreted as mountains when they were really molehills, I would spiral even further. *I can't find the right email address. I don't want to give up Monday nights to do a short course. I want to travel, so I can't afford to do a one-on-one mentorship. I can't be bothered. So and so never had to give up anything for their goals. I don't want to make sacrifices unless I know it's going to work in my favour.* These factors are all justifiable, but when you compare them to how far I go to clog my arteries, how many times I've prioritised a season finale over eight-hours of sleep, it just doesn't add up.

What you spend your time on says a lot more than you think. So too do the lengths you'll go to to rationalise why you don't have what you want.

I can say with confidence that there are at least fifty things I've sworn that I wanted, but the benefit of hindsight has shown me that, in reality, I definitely didn't. I'm telling you this at the risk of ruining my credibility because I know it's important to be honest and open. It's not my intention to come across as a fully self-actualised person who's always known how to apply themself properly. From what I've told you about my personality, you can pretty much gather that I'm a huge ideas-person who wants fast results. I'm not someone who cares about the smartest or the safest way to get a plan executed; I just want it done as quickly as I thought it up. Getting caught up in possibilities is my speciality, and I've never really feared failing because it's easy for me to bounce back and dive headfirst into the next plan. I prefer to work alone and hate asking for help. It wasn't until I reached a point in my career where I had people who wanted to help me bring my visions to life that I realised I could benefit from some assistance. I now have talent managers, a DJ agent and a business partner.

Having manic bursts of excitement for a new idea, only to get over it quickly because I became distracted or bored, was manageable when I worked alone. As soon as I had people on my team who committed themselves to my plans it became clear that I had to exercise some caution. Research, strategise and create with reason!

This style of working hadn't been exhausting or deflating for me because it's my norm, but I hadn't considered how I was impacting the morale of the people I was working with, not to mention their work ethic and perception of mine. I wanted the people around me to understand my process, while at the same time wanting them to feel like they could rely on me to follow through and prioritise things properly. I came to the conclusion that it would be a far better use of my time to apply critical thinking to every idea. Now I'm in this happy grey area where I can execute my outlandish plans (designing and manufacturing homewares for my e-commerce store, making a ReFlex expansion and refurbishing furniture) in an efficient, timely and creative manner. Best of all, a little planning means I'm actually having a higher success rate and seeing things through to the end.

We all have a vice that we've invested more time, money and energy into than our goals. We've all had that moment when we've worked hard on something, only to realise that we don't want it anymore. And there have definitely been other moments when we've gotten everyone excited for our Big Plan, just to later confess we've moved on from it. **It's time that we start identifying the difference between wanting something superficially and understanding the reality of what it takes to achieve a goal.**

FEEDING YOUR VICE

When it comes to goal setting, I keep thinking about a concept that I'm going to refer to as 'mileage'. Ever since I got my own car and driver's license, I've been reflecting on a lot of vehicle analogies. How far am I capable of going to tick something off my to-do list? How far can I, or will I, go before I run out of gas and need to refuel? Generally, when it comes to 'important tasks', I find that my capacity to persevere is so much shorter than how far I've gone to secure insignificant stuff. I'm more likely to Google hundreds of different ways to execute a tricky DIY, but if I get stuck on a synonym while I'm writing this book, I'll get distracted, demotivated and spend twenty minutes on TikTok instead.

In order to remind you that your capacity to persist is way higher than you give yourself credit for, I'm going to challenge you to whip out that notebook of yours and write down your top two vices. Are they online shopping, partying or maybe countless hours on YouTube? Whatever your vices are, I need you to write at least ten examples of the lengths you've gone to fulfil them. What priorities have you shafted in order to feed your vice, and what excuses did you give to justify it? Bonus points if you can recall your motivations and thought processes. You can nurse your wounds afterwards, I promise.

The next time you tell yourself that you can't do the thing you're supposed to be doing for whatever silly reason, reference this list of vices and excuses, and know you can do better.

LACK OF
PASSION

ISN'T YOUR PROBLEM

Passion is defined as:

    i.   an intense desire or enthusiasm for something.

    ii.   a thing that arouses great enthusiasm.

Passion as a word is easily defined, but as a concept it's as open to interpretation as love. Love can be tough, rewarding, sacrificial, soft, unconditional, very conditional, superficial or all encompassing. Love can seem like an elite club, and those who've been granted admission will tell you that it's hard to describe, quantify or qualify but when you know, you know. Passion is similarly elusive. The internet tells us that you know you're passionate when:

you wake up in the morning and you can't wait to start working.

you can't sleep because you keep thinking about the Thing.

your eyes light up and your heart jumps whenever someone talks about your passion.

you can't stop talking or daydreaming about it.

you spend lots of time reading and researching it.

you believe that this endeavour is worth pursuing, even when others would rather have you do something else.

doing it just feels right.

All this being said, the definition for passion varies wherever you look — flick to a different website and somebody will muse that passion is what you make of it. I don't know about you, but to yearn for a career, person, or activity in that constant and all-encompassing way feels like something that's going to take up a lot of my time unnecessarily.

Thus, that rhetoric is frustrating to me, as it tells us that in order to be seriously passionate about something it effectively needs to be your reason for living. Or, at the very least, an uninterrupted flow state that completely energises you; rendering you unaware of how time passes, even when the task at hand is difficult. To me, that just seems like an unrealistic recipe for disaster.

Imagine when you start that new hobby, open that small business or pursue that new person and find it's giving you stress-induced hives as opposed to exciting sleepless nights; you might start to wonder if you're on the right track. Suddenly you're insecure about what you want and, instead of interrogating why that is, you convince yourself that a lack of passion is your problem. When we use what we know about ourselves as a basis for what we want there's a certain sense of synergy; it's an inner knowing that makes you confident that even if you're not feeling like you're on the right path, you can press on.

Passion is definitely cool and I'm so stoked that there are people who've found theirs, but I also want to open up the floor to people who haven't. **I don't want us passion-less folk to feel inadequate or as if we're not completely committed to succeeding because we're able to think about other things.** I don't want this type of thinking to derail us off our path in search of this often-illusive thing. Did we lose it? Did we never have it? Is it real? It doesn't matter. **Your dedication to your goal shouldn't be dictated by how uncomfortable or feverish it makes you.**

We know that what you'd lose sleep over is a good indication of what you'd happily spend your time on. That idea is a tool you can use to help determine where your interests lie, not a compass directing you where to go. Set your own standard of what passion looks like for you. We're not giving the word a new definition, but establishing a few indicators to help you see when you're really interested in something wouldn't go astray. Perhaps you find yourself excitedly thinking about this Thing randomly throughout the day. Maybe you allocate way more hours than you can afford to it (staying up late? Losing sleep? Bludging at work?).

Whether or not you think passion is a myth or you're just turned off by common examples of the phenomena, don't let the definitions concocted by others determine how you find and express interest in yours. It's all relative.

STEP FOUR

Know
you

why want it

WHAT THIS CHAPTER *WILL* TEACH YOU

How to figure out what success looks like to you and why you want it

How to decipher why you haven't achieved what you want yet and take accountability

How to set your intentions, and how intention versus impact intersects with success

How to use the five whys to discern between what you actually want and what you say you want

How to know if your goal is the symptom or the cure

How conforming to traditional ways of success can affect you

How to analyse if you're scared of failing or scared of succeeding

FOUR

WHAT THIS CHAPTER WON'T TEACH YOU

How to set unrealistic expectations for yourself

How to conform, ignoring what you really want

How to dodge accountability and delude yourself into thinking that your mistakes are everyone else's fault

WHAT DOES SUCCESS LOOK LIKE TO ME?

When I started thinking about success and what it looked like to me, I began to spiral.

Success and being successful are concepts people reference a lot in relation to ourselves and others. It's what we crave, what we aspire to and what we stress over. **Having it and pursuing it empowers us, and the lack of it makes us insecure. But what even is success?**

Of course, we have the classic Hollywood approach to success: the expensive sports car, fame, status, privilege, champagne, a huge lavish house and ridiculous amounts of expendable income. But, aside from this type of success not being achievable for most people, is it even relatable? Yes, this is what we've seen and been conditioned to believe is right, but is this what we want?

On some level, I definitely do. I want the house, the car and the nice things, but I also want a ton of other stuff that isn't traditional or conventional. I want to live on a farm, I want to learn how to woodwork, I want to run a business, I want a portion of my life to be dedicated to doing what I want to do and not what I feel obligated to do. I don't want to be forced into prioritising making a living over actually living. Choosing to go down the creative path isn't necessarily a conventional route to success, but it does mean that I can reap some of the benefits of now and avoid the classic 'work hard and have fun when you retire' rhetoric.

It wasn't until I began planning this book that I took the time to think of what success meant to me. Aside from knowing that the definition is ever-evolving, I settled on my theory that success is the combination of trying, doing, learning and achieving. The vagueness of that statement helped me to realise that **success is the process, the journey and the outcome.** I realised it's cyclical in nature, which got me thinking about the effort it takes to attain and sustain success.

What happens after I acquire all the things I want? How do I keep them? Will I be satisfied? Will I want more? Will success get easier with every achievement? Does your capacity to succeed multiply when you're considered successful? These are all questions I'm still figuring out the answers to.

When I moved from full-time to freelance work, I wasn't fully aware of the implications of achieving my goal. Yes, I had expectations of what life would be like once I'd made the transition, and part of me thought it would all turn out exactly how I'd imagined it. I really believed that once I made that change, I'd be working less; making more time for leisure, sleep and my hobbies. Things didn't go exactly as planned. I was so attached to my preconceived idea of what success as a freelancer would look like that I couldn't fathom it might not be my experience. I was working way more hours than before, trying to build a consistent portfolio and client base. I was creating because I needed to live and make an income, not just because I wanted to. While I was technically my own boss, everyone who became a client was also my boss because I was bound by a brief and their expectations. Before I started freelancing, I hadn't processed that if I didn't work, I wasn't going to get paid, whereas in a traditional job I could take a day off, have sick leave or just be a bit bludgey and the money would still hit my account. The biggest shock of all was that I would constantly have to communicate my value and my worth.

All of these things were a very rude awakening for me as they disrupted my fantasy of what it would be like to be a freelancer. Granted, I was in a position where even though getting what I wanted didn't go exactly as planned, the outcome wasn't detrimental. There were still heaps of perks and pros that kept (and still keep) me motivated. What I'm trying to say is that it's super important to understand that in an ideal world your goal is a great thing, but one small change can have a big impact on your future. We need to be aware that with every action there is a reaction, with every positive there is a negative, with every good there is a bad and with every left there is a right. Someone or something is always trying to maintain and restore balance. **You can assume that one change will result in another, and while you might have anticipated that, we don't have ultimate control of everything that happens in the world.**

Keep in mind that when you achieve your goal, what it looks and feels like can be different to what you prepared for: **not everything is going to unfold the way that you imagined just because you want it to.** The reason we prepare ourselves is so we can move towards the outcome we want, not to guarantee anything. That's just the reality of success — sometimes it's closer to what you expected than others. The beauty is in trying, because when things do eventuate like you had planned, it's really lovely.

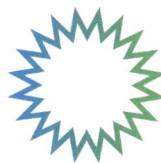

WHAT ARE YOU
WAITING FOR?

Honestly speaking, why do you think you're yet to achieve what you want? What's stopping you? Are there tools you haven't learned or connections you haven't acquired? What's been the barrier to your success or the enemy to your progress?

This chapter will be a huge lesson in taking accountability for yourself and reframing your desires. It's important to see your barriers with as much clarity as possible. This practice will help you to build resilience and ensure these humps can be dealt with when they arise, as opposed to being the things that bring you to a crippling halt.

Read this slowly: **There is a clear difference between superficially wanting something and actually working to get it.** There are so many things I want: a flat stomach, financial freedom, the ability to cook more than three things, patience, more time and an abundance of energy. I don't have those things because I eat processed food daily, spend recklessly, don't enjoy cooking and therefore won't invest time in learning how to make new foods (also see point one), I prefer to avoid people who irritate me, I believe time is a construct and, well, there is no good reason why I haven't gobbled up some iron tablets ...

The point is, I can comfortably air out this stuff about myself because I know it's OK to want something but to not invest time into acquiring it. The problem is when you fixate on these things, spinning tall tales about how you'll do anything to have them, when in reality you're sitting at home watching reruns of a show you hate and avoiding responsibility.

The first step to changing this narrative is to make the distinction between the things you want that you're willing to work for versus the things you want that you'll merely fantasise about having.

WHAT YOU'LL WORK ON
VERUS WHAT YOU WANT

A crucial part of getting what you want is being self-aware enough to know which things you'll actually pursue and which will stay on your to-do list indefinitely. When you know what your priorities are, it's easier to assess what your focus should be. In this activity I want you to be completely transparent with yourself. Make peace with the things you know you want and are willing to work for and accept the things you're happy to have remain as beautiful fantasies. Ask yourself:

What's the criteria for things you plan to do?

What's the criteria for things you want but have no intention of pursuing?

Are there any similarities in the goals you plan to do and the ones you don't plan to do?

What elements would have to change for something on your to-do list to get pushed to the to-never-do list? And vice versa.

INTENTION VS IMPACT

Intention: What you meant to do.

Impact: The result of what you did and how it affected you or others, be it positive or negative.

The distinction between intention and impact is something that comes up a lot in discussions about communication styles. Most of us can recall a conversation where what we've said hasn't been received in the way we expected it to be. You express honest concern for a friend's wellbeing, and they feel attacked. You tell your parents they should paint their apartment walls blue, and while you pictured sky blue, they picked cobalt. Miscommunication happens.

In order to be a strong communicator, you have to understand that the intention behind your words is so important. Being accountable for what you're saying, how it comes across and how it's interpreted is your responsibility. If all those ducks are in order, then the result of what you say will generally align with your expectation.

It's easy to assume that everyone will naturally understand your behaviours, thoughts, actions and words, because you understand those things about yourself. But, if you think back to the amount of times you've been misunderstood in your life, you know that this understanding isn't as inherent as we think. Similarly, when it comes to goal setting and success, understanding your intention versus your impact is crucial. You might have an idea of what you want, which is influenced by your biases and perception. But in reality, the outcome of all the steps you need to take to get what you want might lead to a reaction far different to what you imagined. Maybe it's difficult, unglamorous or a little bit tedious. You could intend for the success you garner to be lush and exciting, but a lot of the time the impact of working hard is ... well ... hard work.

All this reminds me of the Instagram versus reality phenomena, where we're able to see the idealised version of someone's life through the final image they've posted; then we're exposed to the reality of what it took to take that photo, which is either heaps of equipment, someone contorted into a crazy position, or a mess that's been expertly cropped. When we're able to see what that photo looked like without editing, it's often miles away from the final image.

Let's say you've been fixated on moving out of your hometown into the city for years. Your town doesn't inspire you. You're bored, unmotivated and are craving change. Thanks to the internet, you've been able to see what the world is like through the comfort of your own home and that insight has you convinced that you want to move to Los Angeles. It's bustling, vibrant and chock-full of opportunity. You scrape together some coin, take your essentials and waddle to the City of Angels. Within months, LA, similar to your hometown, feels too familiar and doesn't excite you anymore. You're frustrated because you convinced yourself that this shift in location would be the antidote to your lacklustre view on life.

We visualise aspirational situations that are unknown to us with a certain level of optimism and hopefulness, which can often be impacted by our personal bias, conditioning and, more interestingly, fantasies.

We project positive characteristics onto what we want and how we'll feel when we get it. We imagine we'll feel content and whole; after all, this one thing could change everything for the better, right? But you can't fully anticipate what you've never experienced, and while research can help inform your understanding there's still the great unknown. In addition to this, we trust our gut, intuition, or hunches, which are all subjective tools. They're basically the combination of years of habits your brain has been conditioned to recognise as 'normal' and therefore assumes are right or true.

Let's not forget that we're constantly projecting. In the psychological sense, projection is a defence mechanism where people assign their own perceptions onto others. What you believe internally is what you begin to see externally. **When you're wishing for something in particular, it's easy to think one-dimensionally and literally, not allowing yourself to consider the reasons why it might not work out as you intended.**

Let's think about this cycle: We feel a void within ourselves. We have a craving and assume the thing we crave is the answer to the void. We rush to fulfil the craving by any means necessary — forgetting that the void is the real problem — and then feel a spike of dopamine from resolving the craving. Soon after, our dopamine drops and we realise that the void is still there, but now we're hyperaware of it. Pretty soon we have a whole new craving, and hey, maybe fulfilling this one would be enough to get rid of the void!

Let's swing back to the LA example with this cycle in mind. The void was a lack of excitement and a want for spontaneity; the craving was a change of scenery. This person believed that moving would bring them excitement and, while it did in the beginning, the move to LA was only a temporary solution that gave the impression of progress. Dopamine spiked initially from the move but dropped again once everything had settled. I would suggest that this person analyse why they wanted to move and dig down to their real motivation. Using our critical-thinking exercise, we'd ask why and keep unpacking until we got to the root.

I want to go to LA because I want the excitement of a new scene.

Why do you think that a new location is going to be more exciting?

Why do you think LA is the right location for you?

Have you considered other locations?

Why do you think there's a lack of excitement in your life?

To ensure that your goals have a high probability of working in your favour, it's fundamental to figure out your intention. Think broadly about the things you want and start pulling them apart to the most granular form. Imagine that you're an entrepreneur on *Shark Tank* pitching your idea to a panel of ruthless judges — but in this scenario you're not only the entrepreneur but the panel judges too. This is a crucial time to be savage and honest. Can you truly prove to yourself that what you want is valid, feasible and achievable?

HOW TO SET YOUR INTENTIONS

Step one: Think about what you're setting your intentions on and reflect on your experience with this scenario to date. The priority here is to think about your past, as this will give you an indication of how things will play out in your future.

Have you achieved success in this area before, and if so, what helped you do that?

What has stopped you from achieving in this area before?

Step two: Interrogate yourself and ask why you want the thing you want. There is no right or wrong answer; this reflection activity is done so we can determine your needs, motivations and barriers. Look for the reoccurring themes in your answers. They'll give you insight into what you need to work on.

What do you want?

Why do you want it?

Is what you want valuable to your long-term goal?

How do you think it will improve your current situation?

Are your wants sustainable?

How hard are you willing to work for this thing?

Are you sure that this is necessary?

Step three: Set your intentions. This is a simple way of asking you to set a goal with clear justifications as to why you want it. Your intention will ensure your reason for achieving this goal is front of mind. Your intention is allowed to change while you strive for this thing you want, but it's important that you're aware of when it changes, why and if you need to adapt your actions to suit.

USING THE FIVE WHYS

As we've discussed, setting a goal is simple — the real skill is discerning between what you say you want, why you think want it and what you actually want. In order to identify your real goal, you can use the five whys. The five whys are an interrogative technique that explores the relationship between what you want and why you want it. This technique is a way to figure out what the root of your 'failure' so far has been and why you haven't yet succeeded in getting what you want.

In this instance, we're going to use this technique to uncover why you want your goal. As you continually ask yourself why, each answer becomes the foundation of the next question — the idea is that by the time you get to the fifth why, you should be at the heart of what you want.

The point of this is to learn how to troubleshoot your life and avoid one-dimensional assumptions. Even though you may think you have a clear idea of why you want what you do, this exercise should highlight a few areas you didn't know you needed to consider. Don't jump to conclusions or rush to get to the fifth why.

In my experience, the more whys you ask, the better. Aim for no less than five, but don't be afraid to ask more.

I want a promotion.
WHY do you want a promotion?
Because I want more money for the job I'm doing.
WHY do you want more money?
Because I don't like the job I'm doing and I think having more

money will take my mind off it.

WHY don't you like the job you're doing? WHY do you think having more money will take you mind off it?

I don't like my job at the moment because I don't feel validated by my boss and managers. I know I'm good at what I do, but because they don't understand the extent of the job and how hard it is, I don't feel appreciated. I'm overworked, I don't feel supported and I hate that I spend most of my time in an environment that makes me feel bad. With more money, I'll be able to invest into the hobbies I like that bring me joy.

WHY do you feel like investing more money into hobbies will bring you joy?

I spend so much time at work and it depletes me emotionally. When I'm able to do the things I love and enjoy, I feel like a more balanced and happier human. That feels like a worthwhile investment.

WHY will you still stay in a job that depletes you emotionally and doesn't nourish you?

Because I'm insecure that I won't be able to get another role that ticks all the boxes, so it's easy to stay in a place that doesn't.

The last why you answer should point you to a gap in your understanding, a process that's not working well for you or something that you haven't yet considered.

IS YOUR GOAL THE SYMPTOM OR THE CURE?

At this point of our success experiment you'll likely have a good idea of what you want and just need assistance in getting it. To sum up one of the most important learnings from this experiment so far, getting what you want requires self-awareness. The self-awareness to know who you are, who want you want to be, what you want, why you want it, how you'll get it and what will happen if you do.

Let's throw back to when I was working in PR. Among many things, that role wasn't creative enough for me and I felt like a robot going through the motions. My environment was (subjectively) toxic, boring and tiring; all this contributed to my eventual burnout. My career as a DJ was a means to combat that monotony with excitement. It didn't take long for that feeling of boredom and burnout to come rushing back. I was baffled that I could be feeling anything close to bored when I was literally getting paid to play music and facilitate a good time. After some very hectic self-analysis, I came to the conclusion that, despite liking my job and completing my goal, I didn't want to be a DJ.

DJing was my one-dimensional solution to a multifaceted problem. It helped eradicate the feeling that I wasn't getting enough creative freedom in my job, and it helped me with my need to be validated. For a short while I forgot all the things that had been bringing me down from full-time work, I was consciously enjoying myself. But soon the routine started becoming a 'real job', just like the one I had tried so hard to get away from.

I worked night and day and still couldn't fully express myself creatively, as each venue required me to play a certain style of music. Surprisingly, playing thirty hours of nineties RnB for months on end wasn't the best thing for my sanity ... I didn't drink (seriously, I've probably been drunk four times in my life. I don't like the taste of alcohol) and didn't love clubbing when I wasn't part of the party. Most importantly, music wasn't a passion for me, and the presumptuous narrative that it should have been began to plague me.

Do you see the distinction?

It's not to say that I don't enjoy DJing at all, but the biggest thing I learned from that situation was that you need to **be specific about your wants and goals and unpack the motivations behind them.** If I'd asked myself why I wanted to pursue a career in DJing I might have been able to avoid a second round of burnout.

> *Learning what you want shouldn't be an onion that causes you pain and discomfort as the layers unravel.*

Using your self-awareness and checking in with yourself often are easy steps towards making sure you're on the right track to fulfilment.

HAVE YOU HEARD OF THIS CONFORMITY EXPERIMENT?

Solomon Asch was a twentieth-century psychologist best known for his experiments in social conformity. Asch conducted a heap of experiments that questioned how social pressure from a group could affect the extent to which a person conformed or behaved according to social conventions. This concept is called group conformity.

In the fifties, Asch conducted a lab test using male students. He told them he was studying their eyesight (plot twist: he wasn't) to observe if the students could accurately see if lines on a whiteboard were of different lengths. For each group studied, there were ten students who were in on the experiment and one unlucky participant who was being tested.

The experiment was simple: the participants had to sit at a table and were shown a whiteboard that had one straight line on the left side, and three other lines of varied lengths called comparison lines on the right. Of the comparison lines, one was shorter, one longer and one was the same size as the initial line. The students were asked to compare the lengths and determine which of the comparison lines on the right side was the same length as the one on the left. It's important to note that it was super obvious which lines were of equal length as Asch wasn't actually testing the participants' eyesight, but how easily the students could be swayed to think that the clearly correct answer was wrong.

The person being tested sat at the end of the table, and one by one the fake participants said which two lines they thought were equal. The other participants all chose the comparison line that was noticeably shorter than the standard line. Out of the eighteen different trials conducted, seventy-five per cent of the real participants conformed by giving the incorrect answer at least once, while twenty-five per cent never gave in. Asch then flipped the study on its head and asked everyone at the table to share which two lines they thought were equal, but this time all participants were instructed to give the answer they thought was correct. In this group, where there was no pressure to conform, less than one per cent of those tested gave the wrong answer.

After the experiment, those who readily conformed were interviewed, and the findings were wild. Most of them said that they knew their answers were incorrect but had given them out of fear of being teased and ridiculed. The experiments confirmed that when we feel a sense of pressure, we find it easier to go with the norm. It also showed us that people conform because they want to fit in to avoid being seen as the 'other', even if that means going against what they actually think is true. The final reason was because the participants assumed the others in the group were more educated or had insights they didn't have, which made them conform to what they believed was the 'winning' team. This is a good time to honestly ask yourself which group you believe you would occupy more.

Let's talk about Asch's experiment in relation to your success journey. What's motivating you to pursue your goal? Is it that you don't want to be seen as an outsider? Do you lack confidence? Are you afraid to go for what you actually want because of what other people think?

As the study concluded, when people are under pressure, they are more likely to conform to what's normal or easy, rather than staying true to themselves. When there is no pressure, we almost always stay true to ourselves. However, most of us aren't lucky enough to be in environments where we're not influenced by outside factors. This means it's our job to be more self-aware and discern when we're acting in line with what we truly want.

This experiment is not as easy as being given a simple three-step money-back-guarantee guide. It's a deeper analysis into you; you at your core; you, fundamentally. This experiment is asking you to take a step away from how you've been socialised to perceive yourself and to look deeper into who you are, what you want and why you want it.

From the time we were babies to now we've all had certain ideas reinforced. Those who conform have generally been regarded as normal or right, and those who don't are often seen as abnormal or wrong. While it's unusual for people to tell you they think you're an alien for being true to yourself, it can feel like there are unwritten rules in place that keep us conforming to standard ideals. At the very least we can see the benefits of doing what's expected of us; **we're affirmed, praised and congratulated for doing what's always been done, and it can take a huge leap of faith to go against the grain.** It's important to assess whether your dreams have been born out of obedience or if they're truly yours.

There are social norms that are so common we might not even realise how much they influence us.

Breakfast is the most important meal of the day.

People in monogamous relationships are happy.

Wearing a suit means you're professional.

Women are more nurturing than men.

Men are better at driving than women.

Children should be raised by two parents.

Society, media, the internet, the world, the patriarchy, the people who raised you, and your friends will all directly and indirectly influence your behaviour. **Expectations burden us all, yet most of us waddle down the straight and narrow because we think that being slightly uncomfortable with our path is better than being a social pariah.** Social norms are unwritten rules for our behaviour which show us how to act in a way that will cause the least friction. Why do they exist? Probably because humans crave hierarchy and predictability.

Because of all this pressure to conform, it's hard to know where to draw the line between who you are and who you've been conditioned to be. Are your desires even yours or the result of years of external influences? That's tough to answer, in fact, it's almost impossible. I'm not telling you this to propel you headfirst into an existential crisis, I'm telling you this to alleviate some of the pressure.

I don't know how to effectively decolonise my mind. I don't know how to separate myself from who I truly am and who I've been conditioned to be. I don't know how to not be influenced by the societal pressure that tells me to aim for a 'conventional' form of success. I don't know how to fully detach from peer pressure. But what I do know how to do is self-evaluate, ask myself questions and look within for answers that might help me understand myself and my behaviour better.

It's our job to be more self-aware and discern when we're acting in line with what we truly want.

WHAT DRIVES YOU TO CONFORM?

In this exercise, we'll take a look at past and present experiences to understand your relationship to conformity. Reflect on the following:

In your experience, what has caused you to conform?

What has caused you to rebel?

In what environments do you feel pressure to fit in and where does this pressure come from?

Do you feel pressure to conform to social norms? Which ones and why?

Have you ever felt pressure to change your beliefs and behaviours to fit in? If so, which beliefs and why do you think you were asked to think differently?

Recall a time when you encouraged someone else to conform to your beliefs or behaviour. Why did you do this, and were you able to convince them to see your point of view?

What are the implications of not conforming?

After you've answered all these questions, look for common themes that can help you to understand environments where you feel pressure to be like someone else. I'm not arguing that sticking to the status quo is a bad thing, we're just looking for examples of where it can be bad for you. What environments are going to hinder your success, and which will help you thrive?

ANTICIPATING FAILURE: YOU CAN HAVE IT, BUT DO YOU REALLY WANT IT?

A common narrative about aspirational people is that they like to succeed and are scared to fail. Obviously failing has terrible implications, as it can be an upsetting experience.

You put a huge amount of your time, money, energy and effort into something; this preparation leads to optimism and can make us forget that sometimes things don't go to plan.

I've always been interested in what failure does to us psychologically. In an ideal world we can assume that it works the exact same way as our set level of happiness: no matter how shitty, demoralising or detrimental an experience is, we'll eventually bounce back up to our normal level of optimism. But, unfortunately, I don't think it works like that.

We'd be foolish not to consider the psychological impacts of losing. For some it's merely a mindset shift and they're good to continue on their path, but for others, I imagine that failure can have deep, negative impacts on your perspective, thoughts, behaviours and, of course, your resilience. Consider how failure changes your relationship to success. It's smart to understand that failure is a common and unavoidable part of gaining success, so much so that it should only be expected. But how do we prepare for the unexpected?

==What happens when we get our wires so crossed that our anticipation of failure causes us to fear success?==

Is it possible that we'd start inadvertently blocking our blessings because we're scared of the hardship that could be on its way?

SO, WHAT ACTUALLY *IS* FAILURE?

It's a combination of self-doubt, fear of the unknown, underlying inadequacy, pessimism and self-sabotage; all working together to force you into leading a life with insecurity instead of equipping yourself with the tools to manage your situation better.

How failure manifests depends on who you are, your past experiences and your unique situation. For some it's:

The impostor syndrome, a feeling that causes you to doubt your ability and accomplishments. You might see your success to date as a fluke and live in fear of being exposed as incompetent, or worse, fraudulent.

Thinking that you don't have the ability to sustain your progress.

A fear that you'll achieve your goal but still won't be happy or content.

A fear that no matter how much you achieve, it'll never be enough.

A fear of the amount of work needed to sustain a certain level of success.

Fearing success isn't as literal as it sounds. Say I write an amazing book — my publisher is proud of it and it's well regarded by my peers, the media and my social media followers. As exciting as this accomplishment may be, once the excitement subsides, I might start thinking about the pressure of following this achievement. Am I expected to write a second book? What if it doesn't perform as well? And, if I write a second, do I need to do a third? What if I can't think of anything interesting or profound to write about? What if people don't find the next book as interesting and nobody buys it? What if my views change in the future and I no longer believe what I wrote to begin with? This internal turmoil is one of the many negative implications with fearing success. Others are:

A steadily decreasing morale, which causes you to lose all motivation.

Convincing yourself that you no longer want to achieve your goals.

Downplaying and no longer seeing the value in your achievements to date.

Nurturing a negative mindset so regularly that it becomes hard to shift back into a positive one.

Sabotaging, procrastinating, creating reasons why you can't do things or refusing to put in any effort towards your goals.

Failure is an experience that usually happens in private, yet we fear the whole world has front-row seats to our downfall. We avoid failure like the plague, getting crippling anxiety from the anticipation of it, or worse, acting like the failure never happened and pretending we have it all together. The irony is that failure is probably one of the only relatable constants in life. Failure is a feeling and state of being that every person in the whole wide world will experience. And this is where we breathe a sigh of relief.

Didn't Thomas Edison attempt to make a lightbulb 1000 times? Didn't Dyson make almost 5000 prototypes for their iconic bagless vacuum-cleaner? And the thought of failing once has you quivering in your boots?

Have you ever considered that the reason you haven't achieved 'success' yet is because you might subconsciously fear it? The fear of failure has been drilled into us since the beginning of time, but it seems to me that we aren't even really sure what it is we're afraid of.

Hear me out — the definition of failure is 'a lack of success'. It sounds self-explanatory, but plenty of people have no idea what success even looks like to them. Most of us seem to be stuck in a weird stalemate; scared to fail, scared of being unsuccessful, and in the end, missing out on success because we're too afraid to try. All that avoidance of trying inevitably leads to feelings of failure.

Let's imagine the four most common types of people on a path to success.

1. *People who crave success* and recognise that failure is normal. This is the category I fall into most of the time. As an abundant thinker, the questions *How can I have/do/be/acquire more?* are constantly on my mind. But, unlike most, I've accepted the fact that the more I try the more I'll fail, because that's the nature of the universe. Balance, they say.

    It's easier for me to maintain my status as an action-oriented person because I've conditioned myself to understand that failing is a necessary part of the process. Failing is the thing that guarantees you will learn and have the tools required to tackle the project again, next time with better insight. What's not to like?

2. *People who don't try*. Have you ever been so afraid of failing that you decided not to try at all? Look, technically this isn't a terrible strategy, but it's definitely not the best. Think of it this way, you can try to create walls to protect yourself from the perils of failure; you can build them so high that not even the tallest failure-monster could get you. You might feel safe, but

when you finally muster up the courage to leave, those same walls that once protected you are your prison.

I'm sure millions of people have felt this way before. Dodging the possibility of failure in favour of safe mediocrity. However, when we allow fear to stop us from moving forward, we're likely to miss out on some great opportunities.

3. *People who fear success but try anyway.* Picture this: you're a person who's not one hundred per cent convinced they have everything it takes to get what they want, but you're sometimes open to trying anyway. When you see positive results, a part of you feels empowered to keep going, but another part of you wants to quit while you're ahead, just in case you can't guarantee awesome results in the future. Perhaps you're in the habit of making your dreams smaller so they're more achievable and manageable, but this also means you're never quite pursuing what you actually want.

Let's say you challenged yourself to write a fiction novel, but when you started, the commitment overwhelmed you, so you made it a short story, knowing you could finish quicker and celebrate sooner. When you do finish, you're unable to truly enjoy your accomplishment because you want more. The bigger you dream the harder could you fall, so your success comes with an underlying feeling of dissatisfaction.

4. *People who don't try at all.* Self-explanatory, and probably not you if you're reading this book.

UNPACKING YOUR RELATIONSHIP WITH FAILURE

In order to have a healthy relationship with success and achievement, it's crucial to snuggle up to failure (or at least be cordial with it). Failure provides us with an opportunity to learn about ourselves; how you perceive and are affected by it will let you know what to keep an eye out for on your journey to success. Think about the following:

How do you define failure?

Do you think failure is a necessary part of life?

What have you experienced that you would consider to be a failure, and why?

Has your experience with failure stopped you from trying again?

Did you learn anything positive or negative from failing?

If you were to fail again would you handle it differently?

CHECKPOINT
CHECKPOINT
CHECKPOINT
CHECKPOINT
CHECKPOINT
CHECKPOINT

At this stage you should know that it's always good to be realistic about your aspirations. We often attribute certain experiences to certain results, thinking that everything in life is linear and happens as we intended because that's the way we want it to be. A hectic amount of people aspire to travel or make a big move overseas, mostly because of their preconceived ideas of what their dream destination will offer. The issue with that is, like most things, our imagination can stretch too far and make reality look dull by comparison.

If you attach yourself to fantasy and project bias (whether it be good or bad) onto an experience, then you'll be in a constant battle to manage your expectations.

Those who aspire to move overseas might believe they'll have access to cool parties, people, experiences and memories. Wishful thinking is a cute coping mechanism, but the reality is that these changes are pretty unlikely to be generated by a geographical move. You've had your whole life to build habits, and hoping that a move will force you to change or upgrade your life will leave you sorely disappointed. One would argue that if you really wanted to make those changes you would've done so already, and that consolidating those wants into a big pipedream is a recipe for disaster.

This stage of *The Success Experiment* is our checkpoint. In the great words of Queen Latifah's character in *Hairspray*, 'I know we've come so far, and we've got so far to go.' This is the place where I tell you that it's not too late to turn back if you're not ready for the next two steps. Don't stress, you won't be regarded as a failure. If anything, I'll applaud anyone with the self-awareness to admit that they want to take a step back because they've realised that they still:

1. *Don't know* who they are or who they want to be.

2. *Don't know* what they want or why they want it.

There is no rush. Have a think, backtrack if you need to, and move forward if and only when you're ready.

CHECKPOINT

CHECKPOINT

CHECKPOINT

CHECKPOINT

CHECKPOINT

CHECKPOINT

WHAT DOES SUCCESS LOOK LIKE *TO YOU?*

I've had experiences where I'm knee-deep in something I thought I wanted, only to realise I just don't. We've all been there. These moments of realisation have propelled me into a spiral where I was forced to reframe and acknowledge what I didn't want and start to think about what I did.

Becoming a DJ was a strategic move to escape the monotony of my life: the office job that was taxing, and the feelings of falling apart and because I'd wrapped up my self-worth into work I didn't love. I'm not a perfect self-actualised person, I only realised these things in retrospect. At the time, I convinced myself I wanted to become a DJ to share music with the world. 2014 Lillian was so charitable, a real philanthropist (I hope you hear the sarcasm).

I found out the hard way how wrong I was. I was met with success, but it wasn't the success I craved. I didn't know how to check in with myself. I didn't understand my own metrics for success because I'd deluded myself into thinking that I wanted to share music when it wasn't even about the music, it was about a lifestyle, the resources, the assets and the perception of being a DJ. To stop myself from heading down the same path again, I try to avoid latching onto specific symbols of success. Instead, I prefer to check in with myself using questions that were made with my experience in mind.

Why are you doing this?

What plan is this part of?

Do you feel fulfilled, inspired and on track?

What would make you feel happier?

What would make you feel more motivated?

Are you still striking a balance between what you feel obligated to do (bad) and what you feel a duty to do (good)?

Do you feel like you're behaving in a way that's true to you?

Does this goal feel aligned and part of a bigger picture?

What opportunities do you have for growth?

What learning opportunities have come up?

When I mentally answer these questions, I'm left with far more clarity and a second wind of sorts. I'm still a slashie, hellbent on adding more slashes, and in the years I've been writing this book, I've added a few more to my belt. You know I'm a DJ and MTV Presenter, but I'm also:

An interviewer and live TV presenter with Build Series Sydney (a Verizon web series).

Inventor of a critical-thinking conversation card game called ReFlex.

Owner of an e-commerce gifts and games store called Flex Factory.

Co-host of the most versatile, profound and accessible philosophy/psychology/sociology/anthropology (all the -ologies!!!) podcast, *Bobo and Flex.*

Host of my very own Spotify Original podcast, *Flex's Semi-Factual History Lessons.*

With each slash I pick up, I'm closer to understanding what I really want, what feels the most aligned with my goals, what's the most fulfilling and sustainable for me to continue with in the long term. It's nice and eye-opening.

The questions you ask yourself will need to be specific to your situation. Understanding your motivations gives you a blueprint of what you believe success is. Setting goals based on what you deeply desire is the easiest way to keep yourself on track. It's important to be aware of your motivations and to keep them front and centre, let them be your guiding light. Without that self-direction, you'll find it really difficult to self-evaluate, or worse, you'll regard every setback as fatal. Understanding your motivations will also help you illuminate the barriers to your success. As we've learned through this experiment, these barriers are vital to get across, because if you can't see what your blind spots are, you're going to self-sabotage. You've probably done it up until now and will continue to do so if you can't see what things are directly, indirectly, consciously and subconsciously stopping you.

WHAT MOTIVATES ME?

I might sound like a broken record, but I have a theory that if I explain concepts multiple times, I'm giving you more space for you to acquaint yourself with them, which hopefully means you'll find it easier to commit all this to memory.

Motivation is not just an overused buzzword. It's truly the ultimate driving force when it comes to setting and achieving goals. Your motivation initiates action, encourages progress and sustains momentum. It fuels, nourishes and is a really great indicator of when we are on the track. Identifying the feeling of motivation is easy; it's electric, infectious and exciting. However, figuring out what factors inspire motivation within us is much harder. Ask yourself these questions to get a clear indication of what the links are between what you want and what drives you to go and get it.

Are you motivated by praise?

Are you motivated by recognition?

Are you motivated by balance?

Are you motivated by versatility?

Are you motivated by validation?

Are you motivated by security?

Are you motivated by money?

Are you motivated by love?

Are you motivated by family?

Are you motivated by passion?

Are you motivated by the fear of failure?

Are you motivated by the fear of success?

Are you motivated by people perceiving you positively?

Section — Three

STEP FIVE

Chapter Five:
How You'll Get it

STEP SIX

Chapter Six:
What Will Happen When You Do

STEP FIVE

How get

you'll it

WHAT THIS CHAPTER WILL TEACH YOU

Actionable steps to show you exactly how to get what you want

Why it's important to mentally prepare yourself for success

How to check in with yourself

How to focus on the internal things you can change and stop focusing on the external things you can't

The psychology of making habits stick, and how to break the bad ones

Self-celebration, and why it matters

FIVE

WHAT THIS CHAPTER _WON'T_ TEACH YOU

How to cut corners and compromise your wants for the sake of productivity

How to rush, make mistakes and rush some more

How to blame everyone but yourself for your lack of success

How to go full throttle without preparing

NECESSARY
PREPARATION

Hey friend, we are here. This is the point in the experiment where I show you exactly how to get what you want. Everything you've learned up until this now was to equip you with the mindset to win.

With all the work you've done in the last four chapters, I'm confident you've laid a strong foundation that you can start building on. I've given you a ton of resources, but we've literally just scratched the surface on all the things you can learn to improve your mindset, awareness and capabilities. The groundwork is done for now (but not forever), which means that you're ready to move on to the action phase.

In this chapter, I'll be sharing a number of techniques that will help you to achieve your Thing. Use them in conjunction with each other for optimum results. When reading the next few pages, keep these disclaimers in mind:

1. *Prepare to succeed.* You've gotten this far, now is not the time to half-arse it. Adjust your mindset, build your resilience and be confident of a great outcome, but prepare yourself for the alternative. If you're a little rusty on the skills I've taught you, head back and give the other chapters a quick skim-read.

2. *This won't happen overnight.* But you already know this. I didn't apply a timeline to this experiment or guarantee how quickly you'll get what you want, because in reality that's not up to me. There will be internal and external factors that dictate when you'll get your prize. It may happen sooner than

you imagined or could take heaps longer. The more you get comfortable with that fact, the better.

3. *There is no rush.* There is no rush. There is no rush. You've presumably already waited longer than you want to and, to be honest, before reading this book, you probably thought you weren't ever going to achieve your goal. So, before you get caught up in arbitrary timelines and expectations of how long it should take, just know that it will take as long as it needs to.

4. *Get everything out of your head and onto paper.* I, like many, have trusted my mind to hold on to information that I've promptly forgotten minutes later. Don't risk it. Instead of getting frustrated at yourself for doing this, let's focus that energy on a solution. You need easily accessible and reliable reference points for your goals, and studies have shown that vividly describing your goals in written form is conducive to achieving them. Get a noticeboard, use your phone to take notes or pop some Post-its on your fridge or toilet — anything that will help you clearly see what you want and what needs to be done to get it.

5. *Make sure your goals are clearly defined.* As we've learned in previous chapters, this might mean breaking down one big idea into smaller, more manageable goals. We're trading 'Move to Los Angeles' for 'Save fifteen thousand dollars, buy my plane ticket, sort out my visa and move to Echo Park in LA to start my activated-almond business.' Ensure your goal includes what you intend to do, why and how.

Before you head on to the next activity, let's try a reflection exercise. Checking in and drawing comparisons between the past and now can help put your progress (or lack thereof) into perspective. I know you're excited to get to that point of the book where I stop with the chitchatting and start telling you exactly how to get what you want, but I promise you, taking the time to be introspective is just as important.

Throughout this book, I've shared some of the things I believe have been integral to my success journey. I had insecurities about whether I'd even be credible enough to teach you anything, because how did I know if my wins had just been some magical fluke or not? So, we called this an experiment. It took pressure off me to guarantee anything, and it took pressure off you to succeed in a short amount of time.

I asked you to commit to reading this with an open mind and to try every activity, even the ones that didn't really resonate with you. Now you're nearing the end of the experiment, I'd love for you to reflect on the experience in itself.

What has been the most helpful, inspiring or game-changing thing you've learned so far while reading this book?

What hasn't resonated with you and why?

How have your goals changed between the first page of this book and now?

HOW TO CHECK IN WITH YOURSELF

When was the last time you had a basic one-on-one chat with yourself? No, I don't mean playing mental table tennis where you jump between thoughts, vaguely talking out loud or giving yourself a reactive pep talk after you do something mildly embarrassing. I'm asking you to recall a time when you've had a literal, proactive conversation with yourself where questions were asked and answered by you.

Does anything spring to mind?

In the same way you can't know how your friends are actually feeling unless you ask them explicitly, how can you truly know where you're at unless you ask yourself explicitly. Sure, you can draw vague or even semi-accurate conclusions by assessing your mood, body language or heart rate, but why not just go straight to the source for the right answer. **Checking in with yourself is a very underrated activity that can do wonders for your mental health and mindset.** You can do it by simply pausing for a moment each day to ask yourself how you feel.

Are you good? Bad? What's going wrong? What's going right? What's making you happy? What's making you uncomfortable? Is anything on your mind? What could make today better?

Carving out enough time to think and respond is crucial in getting you to the crux of how you actually feel.

Instead of scratching the surface, you can file your thoughts and assess which are minor inconveniences and which actually need to be addressed. I don't know about you, but I'm pretty good at distracting myself from how I actually feel, because sometimes it's just too draining to dig deep. I lean on coping mechanisms and short fixes and wonder why days go by and I'm still feeling irritable and overrun. In my experience, delaying the inevitable check-in and using my vices as Band-aid solutions is enjoyable but definitely not beneficial. Rip off that Band-aid! Sort your shit out!

Now, in relation to this experiment, checking in with yourself is a way to assess that you still want the same things. The easiest strategy I can think to do this is to ask a series of questions that force you to evaluate how you feel in that moment.

If your responses are generally hopeful, pragmatic or positive, then you know you're in the right frame of mind. But if they're coming across mopey, negative or scattered, then you know you've got to nip that in the bud ASAP. Up until recently I used to work myself to the bone, especially when I was feeling down, because I presumed the high of ticking something off my to-do list was reward enough. As someone with a propensity for burnout, this strategy does more harm than good, so now I take a break, recharge and come back when I'm in a better mindset.

After a lot of trial and error, I've come up with a solid list of questions you can ask yourself to check in on your personal and professional goals. You don't need to do this every day, but I would recommend answering these questions in writing as often as you feel you need to (I do this very reactively, generally when I notice I'm feeling stressed, overwhelmed and overworked), and make sure to date your answers to easily reference how you were feeling with the time you were feeling it.

Is there something wrong?

What feels right?

Is something making me uncomfortable?

What's satisfying me?

How do I feel when I think about my current goal?

Do I still want to achieve my goal, and is it a priority?

What was a learning experience for me this week or month?

What are the positives in my life right now?

What would make my life better?

What am I thankful for?

What sparked joy this week?

What responsibility am I avoiding?

What's putting me in a shitty mood?

What do I love about my life?

What do I love about myself?

What makes me feel my best?

Am I holding myself back, and what from?

Is there any negativity I can cut out of my life?

How do the people around me make me feel?

What's inspiring me?

STOP OVERTHINKING ABOUT EXTERNAL FORCES YOU CAN'T CHANGE (although they can and will affect your output)

Ask most people why they don't have the things they want, and I guarantee they'll rattle off external reasons they have little control over. Which is interesting because if you can't change, transform or improve something, then why would you bother placing so much emphasis on it? I guess in some warped way it's a coping mechanism that gives us some illusion of power.

I like to be validated and rewarded just for existing: I love acknowledgement for turning up to work, people who listen intently when I'm speaking or even hearing them tell me 'please' and 'thank you'. When you're praised for doing what's expected of you (cough, bare minimum, cough), doing anything more than what's easy feels like you're going above and beyond. This then means that when you have to apply yourself it can be a burden. If you've always been given pats on the back for just showing up, and suddenly you put in work and you're not getting the internal praise or external validation, then everyone else is the problem and not you, right?

Wrong.

It's a brutal way to look at it, but mincing my words isn't going to help you.

What would happen if we shifted our focus slightly and thought about how we get in our own way? What if we were able to acknowledge the negative or unhelpful habits we possess that affect our ability to succeed, and spent more time managing them? What if we realised that, in order to get what we want, we actually have to try? What if we came to terms with the fact that there won't always be someone to cheer us on when we're on the right track?

Let me tell you, the idea that I might be the one getting in my own way was something that I deeply struggled with. I had the habit of taking full responsibility for my wins but zero accountability when I 'lost'. The thought of it being my fault was something I could barely comprehend. I would look for absolutely anyone to point the finger at in these situations as a way to relieve myself of the responsibility of being the one who let me down. As we've discussed earlier, this is called a self-serving bias, where you think that you're responsible for all the good stuff that happens to you, but blame all the bad stuff on external causes.

When I tell you not to think about the external factors that get in your way, I don't mean that you shouldn't try to understand them or learn how they can affect you. I'm saying that you should put less emphasis on them; but I get that's easier said than done. **Determine what you can control (your attitude, energy, perspective and mindset) and then focus your energy there.**

In March 2019 I started a podcast with Bobo Matjila, fellow influencer and professional opinion-haver. Our show, *Bobo and Flex*, has been described as an inspiring self-actualised group chat. We talk about any and all things in extreme detail. Airing out our informed and uninformed perspectives, insecurities and opinions, but instead of rampant chitchat, we differentiate ourselves from others by trying to use a critical lens. We talk about dating, but instead of tips on how to secure a man, it's about how to rid ourselves of the patriarchal standards we use to navigate the dating world. We're talking about beauty standards, but it's about decolonising our minds and making sure we're not subscribing to standards that are archaic. We're talking about spirituality but we're not saying religion is good or bad, we're talking about morality and ethical code.

The scope and depth of our conversations has given our listeners the impression that we know heaps of stuff, and that we're good advice-givers. It did not take long for the questions to come flooding in and, regardless of the theme, the majority followed the same formula: 'I, a sometimes-flawed person, am in a situation where I'm being impacted negatively. Why are people the worst? When will they change? I've done everything I can, but my efforts are being thwarted by toxic elements.'

Every time Bobo and I discussed these questions, we would lament the lack of context and the emphasis on the shortcomings of everyone else. I would always wonder if people ever used this much energy to constructively critique their own behaviour. You can unpack systemic and environmental flaws all day but understanding them doesn't give us the power to change them. What we can change is how we respond to these things. We should all know by now that changing your perspective has the power to change your results.

WORRY ABOUT YOURSELF

For the next few days, hours, weeks, months, or years — every time you catch yourself lamenting something you can't change — redirect that energy and focus onto what you can do to manage that irritation or concern. See the examples in the table below and fill out some scenarios you've experienced in your notebook.

EXTERNAL	INTERNAL
My Instagram following is not growing as quickly as I anticipated, despite the positive reception and how much content I'm making.	*Continue to* make content that showcases my skills so when the audience comes, they'll see a page that's been nurtured. *Create different* metrics of success to validate me for my efforts. Instead of new followers, I'm going to try to focus on the engagement and sentiment from my existing ones. *Remind myself* that growing an audience who actually likes me and engages with my content is far more important than an audience growing quickly. *Pitch myself* to other brands to collaborate on projects that will expose me to new audiences.

EXTERNAL	INTERNAL
As a freelance worker, it's not unusual for my invoices to be paid late by clients. This makes it hard to get my finances in order.	*Create additional* income streams so I'm not constantly relying on freelancing money. *See what* financial hacks other self-employed people use to compensate for the gaps in their income. *Substitute with* less expensive products. Simple, obvious and helpful.
Your boss has not given you the promotion you were hoping for.	*Ask for* feedback on what you can do to improve your chances of a promotion in the future. *Look for* areas where you think you could develop and upskill in your free time. *Work on* your resilience, and don't be discouraged from asking for a promotion again in the future.

THE PSYCHOLOGY OF MAKING NEW HABITS ACTUALLY STICK

Doing things that are good for you repeatedly and consistently is tiresome. I don't care what anyone says, I find more joy in doing what I like instead of doing what I should. Not everything I find enjoyable is beneficial and I've come to terms with that. I chase experiences that hit the spot and try to dodge anything else like the plague. Stress and effort with no reward — keep that at least five lifetimes away from me! But the one thing I hate more than anything is the feeling of obligation: dragging my feet to execute for the sake of the end result. Yes, I know that the sensation of getting what you want is a cause for celebration, but am I so naive to think that the process shouldn't suck the life out of you? Surely we can find the balance.

I love the thrill of the early stages of an idea: researching, theorising, conceptualising and consideration. And heck, I even love execution ... if it's quick, exciting, invigorating and painless. Unfortunately, most goals are anything but. They can be arduous, gruelling and activate our fight or flight senses. When I'm not operating at my best and my self-awareness is slipping, I default to flight, choosing to procrastinate or run to the next task I know will make me feel good (quickly).

My erratic behaviour aside, I've read enough (and tried plenty of times) to understand the fundamentals of making and breaking habits. With a teensy amount of discipline, you can create new habits that only require a bit of effort to maintain. That being said, if you're hoping to turn into a drill sergeant overnight, I'm definitely not the person to guide you. I, and I'm sure billions of other people, have bursts of positive habit-building, then I relapse into my comfortable pleasure-seeking ways, prioritising comfort over progress, choosing to do what feels good as opposed to what I know I want to be doing, then I spend the next few moments trying to get back to that utopian point of motivation. It's all part of the process.

Your lifestyle is the result of all your good and bad habits. What you do every day, spend your time thinking about and who you spend it with ultimately informs the person you are, and by extension the things you believe, your personality and the way you're perceived by the outside world.

HOW TO MAKE A HABIT STICK

It goes without saying that there is no perfect method for everyone. So, to compensate for that, I'm going to list a few different options you can try on for size. The idea is that if you try one and it doesn't stick, you can try another. Lather, rinse, repeat until you're closer to the end goal.

START EASY: If you're a flaky goal-setter, this is not the time to pick something that requires all your effort. Don't burn yourself out by trying to overhaul your life in one day. If your end goal is to study two hours a day, first make a new habit to go for fifteen uninterrupted minutes, then build on that.

ELIMINATE TEMPTATION (REASONABLY): No one is above base pleasures and many of us can't say no to a distraction. Make your life easier and run far away from the temptations that will stop you from sticking to your habit. If you're wasting too many hours on your phone, delete the apps that are taking up your time. If you know you can't work on an empty stomach, fuel up well before you begin working. If a cluttered space equals a cluttered mind for you, clean up often or get out of the house and into a library.

DO IT DAILY: Consistency is key, baby! It's crucial to actually work on the task daily in some capacity if you want to see results. You don't need you to exhaust yourself and operate at 140 per cent every day, but ten per cent effort over a few months adds up. Bouncing between doing and bludging is not going to help you here. If you want to learn a new language, practise a bit every day. It's harder to form new habits if you're doing a smidge every now and then.

BE TURBO-CONSISTENT: Try doing the task at the same time, in the same environment and with the same intention every day. This creates a trigger that reminds you of the habit, which will help it become second nature.

THE THIRTY-DAY EXTREME SPEED SESSION: It's scientifically proven that all you really need is three to four weeks of committed effort to make a habit stick. If you make it through the uncomfortable initial stages, you can condition yourself to make the habit automatic, which in turn makes it heaps easier to sustain!

YOU WILL RELAPSE, IT'S OK: Get comfortable with knowing that not all of your attempts to improve will work straight away. If you feel like your momentary lapse in motivation is simply due to a mood or a circumstance, then that's cool: try again when you feel up to it.

However, if you pick up where you left off and find that your motivation and drive is steadily slipping, then maybe it's time to reassess. If a habit isn't sticking it's time to ask yourself, 'Is it because I actually can't do this, or that I don't want to as badly as a think I do?' Yes, we can acknowledge that good habits are, you know ... good for you, but if it's not something that you can't keep up, then you need to know when to fold it and put your energy elsewhere.

VIEW IT AS AN EXPERIMENT: There's a reason I refer to this book as an 'experiment' and not a guide — I'm removing the pressure associated with achieving and succeeding and replacing it with a chill energy. **Experiments don't fail, they just have different results that give you new perspectives and ideas to help you form future strategies.**

THE PSYCHOLOGY OF BREAKING A BAD HABIT

By definition, a bad habit is something you do consciously or subconsciously that's considered to be detrimental to your health (spiritual, mental, emotional and physical). Overall, these habits are subjective. They're not inherently negative, but they can often be distractions which steer you away from positive behaviour that would otherwise get you closer to your goal. These habits can be entertaining, debilitating, stress-relieving or conditioned through circumstance. With this is mind, **it's crucial to recognise that even though something is enjoyable, it's not necessarily beneficial.**

The first thing to acknowledge is that habits shouldn't be processed as 'bad' and 'good' — they require far more nuance than that. As we explored in the last section, habits are difficult to both form and break because they are deeply wired patterns of behaviour often associated with pleasure, and as you know, when your brain registers good vibes it tries as hard as it can to keep them coming.

The key to breaking a habit can be understanding the trigger. It's easy to see what the 'bad' action is, but what causes us to do it? What pushes you to procrastinate instead of working diligently on a project? Why do you wear the same three outfits when you have a wardrobe of plenty more? What drives you to binge-drink on the weekend? Why do you scroll aimlessly on your phone, avoiding other responsibilities? It may be stress, but sometimes it doesn't even go that deep.

Your triggers can be situational or environmental. For instance, I associate my apartment with comfort and leisure. Because of this, it can be extra hard to do anything productive at home because I'm surrounded by things that would make procrastinating far more enjoyable. Lillian is my name and inviting distraction into my space is my game. When I walk in, I take off my shoes, light a candle, sit down on the couch, order junk food, start a new project, stop to rearrange my bedroom, get overwhelmed, go back to the couch and waste hours on my phone, eyes glazed over, swiping and tapping with muscle memory. Even if I'm energised, even if I've got far more pressing responsibilities, even when I'm not hungry and even if I've spent the day being entertained, without fail this is what I'll do when I come home. This is how a habit turns into a routine.

HOW TO BREAK A BAD HABIT

Personally, I find breaking bad habits so difficult that I prefer to focus on increasing the number of good habits in my repertoire. Despite this, I have learned a few things about breaking bad habits, and it'd be crazy for me not to pass them on.

What habit do you want to change and why?

Learn how to separate habits you're insecure about (and would like to change) versus habits that are detrimental (that you think you need to change in order to get closer to your goal). Once you've made the distinction between the two, utilise the 'why' we learned about in the critical thinking portion of the book. Keep asking yourself why you want to change this habit until you get to the core of what's motivating you.

If you can't get to the core or refuse to see what your proper driving force is, you probably aren't focusing on the actual problem.

> Bad habits are pervasive: they'll act like baby devils on your shoulder, challenging you every time you try to do the right thing.

They poke holes in your rationale, making you feel like you have a weak resolve, and are an all-round demotivator.

Let's play a game and pretend that I'm the charming little devil trying to keep you on the dark side where bad decisions go to thrive. You've deduced that your bad habit is eating poorly. Your core motivator is to eat healthy and lose weight so you can fit into the jeans you used to wear five years ago. They're your favourite pair, you say.

Enter me, stage left, asking you to consider a few things. What's the point of changing your whole lifestyle when you can just buy new jeans? Why are we placing so much importance on a piece of clothing from half a decade ago? What is the correlation between being healthy, eating well and wearing jeans? It's entirely possible you could eat healthily and not lose any weight. What is the spiritual, physical, mental and emotional benefit of putting all this emphasis on how your skin and fat contorts in this particular fabric item?

Your mind has the ability to be far more critical than I was, because it actually knows your weak spots. It knows what to say to crush your resilience and resolve, and it will take the opportunity because it just wants to have a good time. And to be honest, a lot of bad habits are fun. Fortify yourself, be real and remember that understanding the root of why you want to change is the easiest step in ensuring that you're fully equipped to do it.

A helpful tip is to focus on eradicating the habit without the pressure of a whole new goal attached to it. It could be a good idea to slowly focus on eating less bad foods, giving yourself time to ease in without time constraints or the added confusion of losing weight and fitting into different clothes. Start small, and when you see results, add another goal post. That way, if you crack and start munching on some gummy bears, it's not the end of the world.

Reflect, record and draw conclusions

Your triggers, habits and negative thought patterns really shouldn't be a surprise to you. Spend a solid amount of time trying to understand what behaviours amplify the bad habits, in addition to how they came to be and how you feel when they come out. Get acquainted and comfortable with communicating these parts of yourself so can have control over them (as opposed to them controlling you).

Treat yourself!

As a rewards-based person I'm motivated by positive reinforcement, mainly in the form of gifts. After making changes, give yourself a treat to incentivise working towards your goal. Use the money, time or the energy you've saved from opting out of your bad habit to buy or do something nice for yourself.

Build a plan

Now that you've identified what needs to be fixed, focus on your solution. How do you think life will look without the habit? How much time and effort will it take you to proactively work on this habit? Knowing yourself, what strategies can you put in place to get to your desired result? Break your path down into small, achievable steps. For example, you can't stop procrastinating indefinitely, but you can commit to working in thirty-minute blocks for every task you do or removing distractions like phones and TVs when you're knuckling down. Allow yourself to build up as time goes on, and make sure to track your progress.

Don't remove without replacing

Generally, when people make new habits it's to counteract pre-existing negative ones. This can be problematic when those negative habits provide you with enjoyment or entertainment. If you watch TV to relax but want to stop because it's taking up way too much time, make sure you find another relaxation outlet that you feel is more beneficial — perhaps listening to a fun podcast that's educational and entertaining. Edutainment?

HOW TO GET

WHAT

YOU

WANT

How to get what you want is a combination of everything you've learned up until this point ... and then some. The pages you've read so far were all exercises in building a strong foundation for understanding yourself, which heavily impacts how you approach success and ultimately whether or not you'll succeed. What you do, what you don't, what you should, what you shouldn't, what you can and what you can't do is now information you can comprehend more easily.

One of the very first things I told you is that because you're a unique and complex individual, the steps you take to claim your prize will unfortunately also be as complex as you are. Yes, there are key steps that will overlap for all the people who complete this experiment, but the point is, whether or not you succeed, and how you do it, is all on you. It's your responsibility and your priority; and ultimately, if you don't get it, it's your fault.

I'm not leaving you out to dry, but you've got to understand that I've already invested in your success. I've given you options, insights and a ton of different ways to approach this final chapter. Not everything you've read is going to be the thing that gets you what you want. However, I've done my due diligence and taught you all the relevant information I know, so you have agency to get yours on your own terms. I want you to go out into the world feeling equipped and confident, not reliant on me to continue to fill in the blanks for you. It's up to you to test, trial and combine them in a way that's personalised for you and your goals.

My method is rooted in pragmatism and action. It's the amalgamation of experience, personal failures, observing others, skim-reading books, practising and evaluating. Proceed with an open mind, patience and an abundant mindset. You've come this far.

DISCLAIMER:
Here are the things you should know pretty comprehensively about your goal before you continue. The step-by-step list of how to get what you want is like a recipe, and this checklist is to make sure you have all the necessary ingredients to get through this with as much confidence as possible.

Chapter One Checklist (Who You Are)

A basic level of self-awareness.

An understanding of your personality type.

Your core strengths and weaknesses.

Your values and motivations.

How to self-evaluate to uncover things that you like, fear, dislike and crave.

Chapter Two Checklist (Who You Want to Be)

How to clearly communicate who you are and who you want to be.

Your definition of success.

Understanding the path to success is topsy turvy, and definitely not direct.

How to improve your perspective.

Chapter Three Checklist (What You Want)

What your goal is (ie, the thing that probably drew you to reading this book).

What your intention for this goal is.

Whether your goal is realistic, unrealistic, short term, long term and SMART.

Chapter Four Checklist (Why You Want It)

Why you want this goal.

What you think achieving this goal will do for you.

What's motivating you and preventing you from getting this goal.

Why haven't you gotten this thing yet.

BUILD A
STRONG
FOUNDATION

The strongest foundation to getting what you want is the belief that what you want can actually be yours. I've said it 1000 times in this book, but let's say it again for good measure: **your mindset and behaviour are mostly dictated by your subconscious mind, which stores everything you've ever seen, said and felt.** When I say to you, 'You need to believe in yourself', that's not the beginning of a vague pep talk. It's a reminder that you need to remain vigilant about what you think because it's all being fed to your noggin', whether you like it or not. This is a great time to build mental resilience by improving your perspective and shifting your internal dialogue. Do you find yourself getting sucked into a spiral of negative self-talk when things don't go your way? Does it take you ages to bounce back after disappointing news? Are you constantly anticipating the worst? If this resonates with you, you need to start paying more attention and managing this.

The tools you can use to do this are littered throughout this book in the chapters where we discussed perception, self-awareness, manifestation, positive thinking and the subconscious mind.

But, I digress.

The first step to getting what you want is believing that you can. I'm not in the business of magic, and I can't turn water into wine. If you truly don't think that starting a business, going freelance, monetising your hobby, renovating your apartment, moving to Morocco and learning to abseil is in the realm of possibility for you, then you probably won't do it. And if you really don't think you can, what are we even doing here?

A lack of confidence can be really insidious and exhausting. It's the cold sweat on your palms, the baby devils on your shoulder and that icky feeling in the pit of your stomach. It kicks you when you're down and drags you deeper into the abyss.

Belief is strengthened through a simple formula of: Unpacking what's making you insecure + building skills in the areas you're lacking + practising those skills to increase your confidence = proving you can do it, confirming your ability, building confidence and (best-case scenario) conviction.

As you think about this thing you want, pay special attention to the feelings and thoughts that rise to the surface. Are they positive, negative, hopeful or damning? Once you can clearly define them, you've got to explore why you feel this way. Use the skills I taught you about critical thinking, and implement the five whys to get to the core of your feelings.

LEARN

THE

15 WAYS

TO FLEX

In this context, to 'flex' loosely means to show up, be seen and exceed your expectations and those of others. It's bold and slightly obnoxious, but it fits.

As we've deduced, the reason you don't have what you want is layered, complex and unclear to anyone who isn't you. We've agreed that there are factors you can't control and those you can, and now we have to actually understand what they are. This book has shown you different ways to explore what you need to overcome and conquer to succeed. It could've been your negative self-think, lack of follow-through, inability to commit, debilitating procrastination habit or simply that you've never felt empowered enough to try to change your situation. Now that you've figured out what you want (or, at the very least, you're working towards it), the next step is ultimately the easiest bit: Apply everything you've learned and actually do it. Act. Proceed. Move forward. Go forth.

This is not as easy as it sounds, I know, but there is definitely a process you can implement to help you make progress. At this point, the only difference between you getting what you want and not, is the path you take. **Having a clearly defined route leaves less room for doubt, and most importantly, mitigates how the fear of the unknown will wreak havoc on you.**

The hardest part of achieving your goal is figuring out what steps to take. This is where I come in. I developed an action plan called the 15 Ways to Flex. It didn't need a name, but it helps it sound more official, and I guess it makes it easier to reference.

'Hey, have you tried the 15 Ways to Flex?'
'I'm halfway through the 15 Ways to Flex.'
'The 15 Ways to Flex is honestly the chicken salt to my hot chips.
I need it, I love it, I have to have it.'

Those are a few fake testimonials that I know will be real once enough people have read this book and applied my method.

I've said in 1000 different ways that the path to success is convoluted and anything but straightforward, but surely there's a way to make it more direct, right?

Yes, there is.

My aim is to take your big goal and make it achievable by recognising significant milestones and then by breaking it down into fifteen bite-sized mini goals that can be done daily or weekly. Aside from just liking the way it sounded, (alliteration, you know!) the fifteen steps in my plan are enough to ensure you're really invested in your goal, and that you'll truly exhaust all opportunities to get it.

Gone are the days when we tricked ourselves into thinking that what we wanted was going to be easy to get because it fit cleanly on one line in our notebook. Gone are the days we overwhelmed ourselves and ended up confused and demotivated by not considering that broad wants like 'start a business' or 'lose ten kilos' would take more than one simple step.

Here is a summary of how the 15 Ways to Flex works. Next I'll take you through the comprehensive details.

Choose your main goal: You've identified the thing you want. You're motivated and inspired to pursue your goal, and achieving it will likely mean success for you.

Break your goal down into five milestones: These are the five major things that need to be done in order for you to achieve your goal. This a great technique to help you get more clarity on the task at hand — it helps you prioritise. Spend less time feeling swamped by how much there is to do, and more time figuring out how to do it, I say!

Break each milestone down into fifteen distinct steps: these then become your instructions. Using a bit of imagination, common sense and both objective and critical thinking, you'll create a bespoke list with fifteen points. Made by you, for you, solely focused on getting you towards your goal. The huge list you end up with becomes a step-by-step guide to getting what you want, by ensuring you exhaust all possible opportunities to get it.

Once broken down, start actually doing the things you've written: Your aim is to tick things off the list; this acts as a literal and visual representation of your progress. The list, and your progress through it, also clearly presents what tasks are crucial to the completion of your goal.

Completing all the steps (translation: the five milestones and their fifteen steps are finished) can mean a few things:
- You've completed your goal and found success, meaning you've also completed the experiment!
- You haven't completed your goal, meaning you either need to re-evaluate your milestones or the segmented steps. Learn from this experience. Try to pull out some meaning from all the effort you've put in, and the results you've achieved (despite not winning The Big Prize). What resonated with you and what didn't? How would you approach this challenge differently knowing what you know now? Use this insight to tackle the goal again by creating new milestones.

DEFINE YOUR GOAL

Of course, step one is to define your goal. What do you want, why do you want it, what it will feel like when you get it and what are the non-negotiables for you. For more details on how to do this, jump to page 248 for a refresher on how to write a SMART goal. Once you've done that, go the extra mile and visualise the goal. What will it look like, what it will feel like and even all the ways you believe it will improve your life. Get detailed! Be specific! Be particular! If conjuring up mental moods and imagery isn't your thing, create a physical or digital mood board with illustrations or photos to increase how real it appears.

Jot it down as bullet points, write it in a long paragraph, put notes on your phone or a whiteboard — wherever you can to look at it often. It needs to be comprehensive and clear because this isn't the time for ho-hum vagueness.

Example: *I want to start my online clothing store. I'm ready to improve my business acumen and build a successful empire for myself, instead of building up someone else's. I want the opportunity to utilise my passion for fashion, money and design in the same place. Creating and stocking garments that I would wear, in addition to stocking plus-sized womenswear, is a non-negotiable for me.*

SEGMENT YOUR GOAL INTO MILESTONES

Let's get this straight — achieving your goal could take way more time than you expect, which sucks to hear, but it's the truth. It's not because you're slow to act, proficient in procrastination or the odds aren't in your favour. It's my personal observation from existing in a world where I've seen (and experienced) that wanting stuff and applying yourself doesn't automatically equal a timely result. These things don't just happen overnight and, if they do, the likelihood of that occurring is so rare that I wouldn't recommend you keep your hopes up.

A good quote to remember is 'Goals define where you're going, and milestones let you know if you're actually getting there' (Christian Fisher, Hearst Newspapers, 2020). Of course, when thinking about your goal, you should be as optimistic as humanly possible, but I think that injecting a dose of realism will remind you to be malleable and fluid. Hope for the best but expect the worst. **Prepare for all outcomes, even the ones that you don't want, because it is possible that things won't happen in the way you foresee.**

Learn how to manage your expectations. We're all in some ways soft, sensitive people with often finite emotional resources — a lot of us can't afford to get knocked down time and time and time again. There is a point where the weight of failure becomes too hard for even the most confident person to bear. What we want to avoid is you peaking because you're anticipating all goodness, hoping for the best and not preparing for anything otherwise.

Getting your hopes up and expecting good news way sooner than it comes is a sure-fire way to annihilate your morale. You've got to keep building resilience — think of it as the safety net your mind is crocheting to protect you if you fall. Imagine what happens if you ride the high of delusion to the top of the mountain and experience a slight misstep that feels impossible to recover from. You fall and have no metaphorical net to catch you. It's going to take a little longer to heal from the bumps and bruises, right? I say all this to say, **leave room for satisfaction and not perfection.** Your priority is getting what you want but appreciate that it could take longer to find joy in the experience.

I, for one, am not interested in delaying gratification until the end, so I recommend setting milestones. This involves segmenting your primary goal into smaller goals or, as I like to call them, accomplishments.

Hitting a milestone:

indicates progress — if you've reached a milestone it means you're doing the right thing.

gives you a reason to pause and take a break so you don't burn out.

provides an opportunity to reflect on what's been completed and see if you're still on track.

provides an opportunity to self-evaluate and see how you're feeling about the goal (think about your emotions!).

marks a time for self-celebration.

Throughout this book I've told you not to focus completely on external factors (because you can't change them), but it'd be remiss of me not to remind you that they will impact you (whether you like it or not).

Imagine saving up money, selling your belongings, and applying for a visa to move to LA. You hop on a flight, stay until your visa runs out and now realise you want to live there long-term. Well, the only way you can feasibly do that is through becoming a US citizen, but you can't because you need a green card and the only way for that to happen is through the Diversity Visa Lottery. A lottery?! A randomised process of basically drawing names out of a hat. There's very little you can do to improve your chances and now your future is left up to fate.

Such is life.

But that's no reason not to try or get excited by the possibilities. Yes, getting what you want is the riveting bit, but if you do it right (using my method) then the process can be just as hype. Little wins left right and centre, fuelling and motivating you until your inevitable big win.

You might be thinking, is this necessary? (Yes.)

Do I really need to sugar-coat the experience with little metaphorical trophies to keep morale up? (I think this is a rhetorical question.)

Am I just distracting myself with these unnecessary tasks, wasting time and energy when I could be focusing on the big picture? (Short answer is, no.)

Let's use my starting an online clothing business example as a reference. There are lots of different areas within that one goal that need to be worked towards separately, like puzzle pieces. Of course, the puzzle is technically finished when all those pieces are laid in the correct spot, but what about that feeling when you've finally completed the perimeters (yay!) or the corners (exciting!) and then the middle bit (weee!!). These are all points that call for celebration, right?

Exactly! So, using that same framework, I encourage you to think about some key points of your main goal.

What major tasks need to be done to help you reach the finish line?

What parts of the process do you have to nail down so that the big picture is seen more clearly?

Is the completion of one milestone contingent on another part being finished first?

When you've got your key parts sorted and have a really good idea of what needs to be done to get to where you want to go, you have to write down five major milestones for your goal. More is always encouraged, but you can absolutely under no circumstance write down less. This is not the time to cut corners. If this feels over the top, prepare yourself because there's a lot of more work (and segmenting) to be done.

For an e-commerce clothing business, here are some things I'd list:

Building a functional website.

Having clothing to sell.

Nailing down shipping and the fulfillment process.

Getting your finances and legal stuff in order.

Getting your branding sorted (logos, colour guides and a business name).

A clear, straightforward structure makes everything seem a little easier, but also way more realistic. Yes, it may be overwhelming to see your goal presented to you in this way, but the more acquainted you are with what it's actually going to take, the better. These steps are what needs to happen so you can get what you want. Practical and actionable. There are no ifs or buts. These milestones also need to be written down digitally or physically to reference later.

Like I mentioned earlier, reaching these milestones is a perfect time to assess your progress so far.

Are you still interested in fulfilling your main goal?

Do you need to adjust any component of your goal? If so, what?

How has the process been to date?

What have you learned about the project?

What have you learned about yourself during the journey to this milestone?

What are we celebrating?

Do you need to add any more milestones?

Do you need to make any adjustments to your plans?

Did any unseen complications arise? What were they and how can you avoid them in the future?

But, first of all, I need to show you how to reach these milestones, right? Yes. Well then, let's move right along.

SEGMENT YOUR MILESTONES INTO ACTIONABLE STEPS

Now that we've cemented what you want and the map you'll take to get there, we need to create the path. You might be thinking, 'How do I know how to create these steps? That's why I'm reading this book, so you can tell me.' And I will. If the steps to achieving your goal or dream were obvious or within your reach, then you probably wouldn't have picked up this book. One of the main reasons I created this action plan is to demystify what hard work looks like. It doesn't have to be vague, extremely overwhelming or for people who are just 'blessed' — **success can be practical and doable, especially when you're the one creating the strategy.**

What I'm about to show you is one of the tools I attribute a lot of my success to. Although I'm confident in my ability, and my mum thinks I'm exceptional, achieving all I have is not because I'm the best or because I've been inducted into the illuminati. It's because I try. I have a way of pushing through, finding different approaches and exhausting all opportunities before I consider a goal a dead end. **I nurture and improve my mindset, which helps me to avoid the roadblocks that come when I'm feeling insecure.** But, most importantly, I'm realistic about what I can actually do.

I've learned my skills, strengths, weaknesses and capabilities. I research and study as many elements of my goal as possible, so I have the best idea of what it's going to take, and then I prepare myself accordingly.

A good example of this is when, one day, I decided I was going to be a beauty influencer. My plan was to make at least a quarter of my money in this space, because I wanted to diversify my income and take financial pressure off myself to work whatever DJ or TV gig came my way. Having the additional coin coming in meant I could work towards saving, being more financially free (translation: having the room to spend more recklessly) and building my brand recognition through partnerships with renowned corporations. From working with influencers in my PR job, I was already aware of how much they could make and the opportunities they were offered. At the time I was the go-to DJ for a lot of fashion and beauty gigs in Australia, and I'd built great relationships with agencies who represented some of the brands I was interested in. And, by that point, I'd already built an online platform, so it wasn't as if I was starting from scratch.

Once I'd decided on my new goal, my initial reflex was to barrel straight into the inbox of my contacts to see if they could help me become an influencer, but I stopped myself. That method contradicted how I'd been teaching myself to approach goals (with my 15 Ways to Flex). It was one-dimensional, putting the results first and strategy second; one of the main reasons I'd burnt myself out in the past. Rushing towards completion by any means necessary meant that I wasn't actually contemplating what needed to be done. I would act recklessly, hoping what I wanted to do would get me results and leaving them up to chance.

I knew what my goal was and I had a good idea of what milestones to segment it into: get on PR lists, get paid work with five major brands, have my work reposted on the brands' social media and go on a paid brand-trip. Now I just had to figure out my plan of attack, which of course included emailing contacts, but I considered a ton of other important things that I absolutely needed to know and have before any conversations were started.

I understand that invigorating feeling of finally zeroing in on what you want. It's electric! You feel this metaphorical high buzzing through you, and you want to go, go, go! Act, do, proceed, progress — by any means necessary! Keep that energy, you're going to need it to maintain your morale, especially in tougher times, but get your ducks in order before you waddle into the unknown, unequipped yet expecting the best outcome. What you need to learn is how to channel that enthusiasm into a more realistic way of navigating goals. One that doesn't drain you or set you up for failure.

Creating actionable steps is just a fancy way of saying you need to figure out what things to do to reach one of your milestones. And yes, trying to work out how to do something you have never done before feels like it's verging on the impossible, but it's not.

It requires a few things:

Imagination — learn how to form new ideas and concepts using your mind, instead of relying on what you have already seen or experienced.

Critical thinking — learn how to see as many sides of an idea as possible using objectivity.

Troubleshooting — learn how to become a problem solver. See the opportunities, find solutions and think deeply!

Application — learn how to apply yourself, and although that's feedback I've been getting consistently since high school, it took me until my twenties to really discover what that is in practice. To apply yourself means to work hard at something, putting in extra effort, to improve yourself or your skills. It requires diligence, focus and the belief that you can.

Let's get into it. Take the five or more milestones that you listed earlier and separate each out into its own heading. Beneath those headings, write down a minimum of fifteen different things you can do to help you reach that goal. The challenge is to think granularly; your aim here is to create specific and uncompleted action points. This is the time to be as literal as possible in your approach. Create a comprehensive list that acts as a step-by-step framework, showing you exactly where to start and how to pivot if you hit a roadblock. Prioritise things that absolutely must happen in order for the goal to be completed, followed by what should happen and then what issues could occur. The more things you write, the more prepared you'll be for all the possible outcomes. Throughout this book, I constantly reiterated how important it is for your goal to be pragmatic and achievable, so that when the time comes to fulfil it, the hardest part is how to approach it. This list takes care of the how, which means your responsibility is to act, assess, learn, reassess, apply, and evaluate until you have what you want.

As you tick off each item, you have to replace it with another complementary task. This ensures that with every bit of progress, you avoid stagnancy by encouraging your mind to continue to be agile and consider all aspects of the goal. What other possibilities can you consider? What other approaches are there?

By the end of this task, every possible avenue you can feasibly take should be thought of. They don't need to be written in any particular order, but you do need to get as many ideas onto the page as humanly possible. Consider everything.

BUILDING A FUNCTIONAL WEBSITE	HAVING CLOTHING TO SELL	NAILING DOWN A SHIPPING AND FULFILLMENT PROCESS	GETTING YOUR FINANCES AND LEGAL STUFF IN ORDER	CREATING A BUSINESS MODEL AND GETTING YOUR BRANDING SORTED
Come up with a website name. This should be consistent with your company name.	Interview people within your target audience to see what they want from an online clothing brand.	Decide on a shipping provider and speak with an account manager to gain insight into shipping processes.	Register for an ABN.	Research your target audience and competitors.
Buy the domain. Make sure to secure this across emails and social media also.	Contact a fashion wholesaler to discuss what garments you want to stock.	Research shipping prices, and factor them into your online sales costs.	Register for a business bank account.	Audit your competitors' site. What do you like and what would you do differently?
Compare popular website developers and choose the one which best suits your needs and budget.	Order your first batch of clothes.	Research and purchase packaging to suit your needs.	How much will it cost you to run this business? What costs do you need to be mindful of?	Narrow down your unique selling point and create your business model.
Using a consistent brand look and feel, take photos of your stock and write product descriptions and website content.	Get the inventory organised and stocked, making sure everything's clear and easily accessible.			Choose the visuals of your brand (colour, fonts, logo, vibe), and use this to design your logo.

Once you complete every cell, you're left with a very clear vision of what steps to take right now to achieve your goal, which is a huge advantage and gamechanger. Remember when I talked about the Johari window, the self-awareness tool? The aim of that exercise was for you to minimise what you don't know about yourself through self-exploration, thus making the quadrant of what you know about yourself much bigger. Consider that approach when doing the 15 Ways to Flex. By increasing your understanding of what it takes to win, you minimise your blind spots and failure due to the unknown.

The list that you made is by no means exhaustive. You've only written down what you think needs to happen, based on what you know. As you complete each task, what you know increases, which means that the list will need to evolve to make room for new ideas or adjust current ones. That's the beauty of it. The list gives you insight to move forward with intent, guided by confidence and an inner knowing. It motivates you to continue, because with each small win you get a small taste of what it will be like to reach your goal.

In the first chapter of the book, I told you that this self-development experiment will eventually call on you to be entirely autonomous. **My role is only to instruct you on how to solve your problems, and now that you've been given the guidelines, it's your responsibility to apply everything you've learned.** The information in this book is just the scaffolding; it's a temporary structure that works as a support system. Scaffolding doesn't stay erected forever; eventually, it becomes a structurally sound building with electrical wiring, plumbing, concrete, brick and décor, and the bare bones are no longer visible.

This book was never going to contain an exhaustive list of every possible goal and all the intricate ways they could be achieved, because it's not necessary or realistic. **Your goals should be as unique and individual as you are — based on your specific motivations, wants and desires.** You're at a point where you understand how success works, conceptually, theoretically and now in practice.

Apply it to any new situation if you hit a point where you feel like you don't have the information you need to succeed. Think! About! It! Use your brain. Challenge yourself to prosper without anyone's assistance. After all, even the most successful people are just winging it.

And that's how you get whatever you want.

STEP SIX

What will when

CHAPTER SIX

happen

you do

WHAT THIS CHAPTER *WILL* TEACH YOU

How to mentally prepare for what happens once you achieve the Thing

How to mentally prepare for what happens if you don't achieve the Thing

How to evaluate an experience to see the benefits

Failure is common and an inevitable part of the process

Action doesn't mean you get what you want; it means you're on the journey

The maintenance of dedication

How to get back on the horse

A call to action to share what you know — there's no value in being the exception to the rule

SIX

WHAT THIS CHAPTER *WON'T* TEACH YOU

How to define yourself by your goals

How to define yourself by failure

How to disregard the effort you've put in because it doesn't match your outcome

How to regress

We did it! You committed to and completed a three-hundred-and-something-page quest to demystify success — what it is to you, why you want it and how to get it. I have a few more pages of excellent wisdom to impart to you and then I'm going to love you and leave you. While the book is almost finished, your journey has quite literally just begun. I don't expect you to dive headfirst into the Fifteen Ways to Flex just yet, because I imagine you'll need time to truly digest and grasp everything you've learned so far. It's your responsibility to figure out how to apply it best for your individual situation. Not every task or activity was made to be used in conjunction with another at all times — the magic is in your ability to know these skills exist, and to use them when needed.

I told you why I called this book an experiment rather than a guide or an instruction manual. I didn't promise you that you'd get whatever you want or that it would be given to you just because you want it. My intention was to give you a blueprint and the tools to do it yourself. To teach you how to take accountability and demand success on your own terms. After all, this is a self-help book, not a genie in a bottle. How effective any of this could be is largely based on the effort you put in.

In creating this experiment, I wanted to take the pressure off absolutes and imperatives, and instead allow you complete agency to do what you wanted with this information.

Through my five years in the entertainment industry, doing cool stuff, giving advice and kicking my own personal goals, I observed that most people wanted to know the same thing about my career. 'How did you do it? What tips and insights do you have and what easy, actionable steps can you share?' Having this book as a reference point for all of that is going to be a gamechanger. At one point, I tried responding to each Instagram DM asking me to condense years of experience into a concise message, but it was literally not possible (and it doesn't pique my interest, lol). To all the people who've been waiting on me to share my learnings, it's finally here. I promise my silence wasn't a weird attempt at gatekeeping. The scope of success is so vast and unique to everyone, that creating this bespoke experiment, which you can consume at your own pace, really is the best way to disseminate this info.

It goes without saying that not only is writing a book hard, but trying to recall the minutiae of my career in detail and relay that in an interesting, insightful and helpful way is one of the most difficult things I've ever done. I'm a pretty confident person but, with every edit I submitted, my confidence crumbled. I started this process with the hubris of a highly motivated girl with nothing to lose (famous last words, lol) — all I had to do was recount, right? But what if I forgot something? What if I missed something vital? What if I'm not helpful? I wildly underestimated what it would actually take to teach without the blessing of immediate feedback. I'm so used to interacting with my audience via IG or on a podcast and receiving real-time commentary on what people need more info on or what I can clarify. But, in this instance, I've stewed over this for years, hoping that when it was finally finished it would have everything you need to get the Thing you want.

Boy, has this book been a process, a great one — often draining, but extremely career-affirming. Overcoming self-doubt, sprinkles of impostor syndrome (that's a new one for me), and the underlying belief that I wouldn't be able to properly help anyone with my lessons, has been a huge challenge. After all, this is an experiment, and the only way to know if this works is for me to publish this book and wait for you to read and apply everything I teach. But hello!! Look at me go, I wrote it and you're reading it and that's such an incredible feat.

I've designed and conducted my experiment in order to accept or reject my initial hypothesis: that you'll be able to achieve success by reading this. To know if my theory is correct, I need your feedback. Like I said earlier, I'm so used to interacting directly with my audience, which means that I've conditioned myself to expect feedback of some sort instantaneously. A like, a comment, a share, a retweet, something! While I realise it'll take a hot moment for you to get this book, read and apply it, I would still love to engage with you during the process and also afterwards when you've achieved your goal. If this experience was helpful to you in any way, I'd love for you to reach out and tell me all about it. What you loved, what clicked, what took a second to resonate with you and even what you hated.

The main thing I've discovered is that success is a mostly a feeling, a habit and/or a journey, made by you, for you. Though your definition of success will often be impacted by external factors, how much it fulfils you will depend on whether you create goals for internal satisfaction or external validation. It's absolutely not a destination because you will never 'arrive'; it's an inner knowing, and a certain level of contentment that comes with the ability to commit to and conquer all the things that have been barriers up until this point.

Success is ongoing, ever-evolving, and a subject you will spend your lifetime trying to truly understand. Every time you tick something off your to-do list and exceed your own expectations by actually getting what you wanted, you'll find you want more and more and more and more and more. Because of this, achieving is a slippery slope. Doing cool stuff makes you happy but pining for more gives you an increasing awareness of what you don't have, which then makes you dissatisfied with what you do, thus making you unhappy. It's kind of human nature, right?

Old-school French author Alexis de Tocqueville has a quote that's pretty profound and eye-opening. He discovered when travelling through America in the early 1800s that he'd 'seen the freest and best educated of men in the happiest circumstances the world can afford; yet it seemed that a cloud hung on their brow and they appeared serious and almost sad, because they never stopped thinking of the good things they have not yet got.'

Of course, this isn't to turn you off from wanting more, but to provide context for what it can feel like when you eventually meet your goal, or in some cases when you don't. From what I'm learning about life, there will never be a time where you don't need or want something. Your job is to make sure that while you're barrelling down this path of progression, you don't forget to look after yourself in the other moments. Make sure your cup is full and your mind is healthy and happy. Self-development and self-betterment are inherently intertwined with scarcity and lack. After all, to be aware of all the ways you can improve is to know all the ways you could be better. Similarly, **to think about all the things you can work towards is to realise all the ways you aren't there yet.** The aim is not to spiral into an existential crisis or to spook you into fearing success, but to remind you to be present throughout your journey. Be mindful, self-aware and attuned to what you're feeling and why, what you're doing and why, and what you're saying and why.

I want you to remember that the arbitrary timelines you intertwine with your ideas of success are only limiting you. **Time should be used as a tool for accountability that reminds you to keep progressing, rather than one that shames and frustrates you.** Telling yourself that you should be at this milestone because of your age or how long you've been working on a particular task only serves to stress you out. Give yourself some grace. Life is hard enough without us breathing down our own necks.

Learning how to express gratitude and appreciation for what you have and what's on its way is a good lesson in keeping your success in perspective. Life is one big experiment and we've only just scratched the surface with this book. As you go forth into the big bad world, wanting things and learning how to apply yourself to achieve them, I encourage you to check in with yourself, revisit the experiment, look over your activities and re-read sections when you need them.

EVALUATING YOUR EXPERIENCE READING THIS BOOK

Learning how to evaluate yourself, your wants, mindsets and behaviour has been a cornerstone of this experiment. The main benefit of getting your thoughts onto the page is that you can make proper judgements and improve your future decisions.

I want you to take some time to think about your progress through this book, mostly because I want you to be able to contextualise your growth. You've learned and experienced so much, and I really think that comparing your ideas from before this experiment to after can teach you a lot about yourself. Use this information to help you with future projects. It's all about staying accountable and keeping the momentum up.

With that being said, here's my final activity for you, to top off your own success experiment. Take some time out and reflect on these questions.

What were your expectations for this book (you can swap out 'book' for project, new business ventures, new experiences, etc.) before you picked it up (slash experienced it)?

What did you think you were going to learn?

Recall three things you've read that changed your life.

What three major things have you learned about yourself?

How did your idea of success evolve?

What new skills and activities have you integrated into your life?

Which part of this experiment was the hardest and which was the easiest?

When you finally achieve your goal using the 15 Ways To Flex (or when you feel as though you've exhausted all opportunities and still haven't gotten what you want), come back and read the last few pages of this book, reflect on the experiences you've had, take some time to celebrate how far you've come, and when you feel ready (don't rush!) plan and consider your next goal!

SO, YOU DIDN'T DO IT?

While you may not have achieved that goal you were after, it's not entirely true that you didn't succeed at all. By investing your time, money and energy into participating in this experiment you've achieved:

A better understanding of yourself, your motivations, your relationship to success and failure.

The ability to identify characteristics and traits needed to be in a better position to grow.

Skills to identify what you want and why you want it.

A framework to create actionable steps to get closer to what you want.

So, therefore, I would argue that success has been obtained. Perhaps not in the way that you'd imagined or prepared yourself for, but that doesn't mean there's no value in the effort you've put in so far. While you haven't gotten exactly what you want, this experience has definitely provided you with resources you can use forever.

This is the perfect time to remind you that 'failing' doesn't mean you are a failure. It's not an indication of your effort or commitment to progressing. It sure as hell doesn't mean you didn't try. It's a sobering reminder that sometimes we can't get what we want just because we want it. Unfortunately, that's just the way life is. We can apply ourselves until we've exhausted all options and still not 'succeed' because we're not the only ones deciding our fates. There are external factors like people, relationships, timing, status, society, glass ceilings, upbringing, patriarchy, intergenerational trauma and nepotism. It's also worth mentioning that even when you're able to do all the things, failing is still a part of that journey. It's unavoidable. Your goal now needs to be to assess how you're going to let this impact your ability to be resilient. Are you going to give up or are you going to take a break, lick your wounds, recalibrate and get back on the horse? I know what I'd do, and I know what I'd recommend.

Saddle up! Don't let an inescapable outcome be the death of your morale and self-esteem. Try again and keep trying until you find your success!

YOU DID IT!

Now the experiment is actually complete. Hello!! GOOD ON YOU!! This is beyond exciting for heaps of reasons including (but not limited to) the following:

It proves that anyone who reads this book, learns what I teach and then practises what they learn will succeed.

It proves my method is legit (hehe). I mean, I've used it and you've used it successfully. That's at least two confirmed wins. The odds are in our favour.

It proves to you that there is a combination of clear, actionable steps that can help you get whatever you want.

It proves that mindset, perspective and behaviour are huge factors that will either inhibit or improve your chances of success.

It proves that you do have the ability to change your situation, if you really want to.

I don't know if you can tell, but I'm on cloud nine. I'm gloating. I'm excited. This is just the best. Now, all you need to do (if that is what you wish) is identify more things you want, and use this formula to keep getting them. Or you could take a break and revel in your accomplishments. Whatever you choose, it would be an awesome idea to pay it forward and pass this book on to someone who might benefit from it.

You're amazing.

We're amazing!!!

Go forth and conduct the next phase of this experiment called life.

Books:

- Rhonda Byrne, *The Secret*, Simon and Schuster, London, 2006
- Charles Duhigg, *The Power of Habit*, Random House, New York, 2012
- James Clear, *Atomic Habits*, Random House, London, 2018
- Mark Manson, *The Subtle Art of Not Giving a F*ck*, Pan MacMillan, Australia, 2016
- Sarah Knight, *The Life-Changing Magic of Not Giving A F**k*, Quercus Books, London, 2016
- Simon Sinek, *Start With Why: How Great Leaders Inspire Everyone to Take Action*, Penguin, London, 2011
- Florence Littauer, *Personality Plus: How to Understand Yourself by Understanding Others*, Baker Publishing Group, Michigan, 2011
- Jonathan Haidt, *The Happiness Hypothesis: Putting Ancient Wisdom to the Test of Modern Science*, Random House, London, 2021
- Don Miguel Ruiz and Janet Mills, *The Four Agreements*, Amber-Allen Publishing, California, 2011
- Gretchen Rubin, *The Four Tendencies: The Indispensable Personality That Reveal How to Make Your Life Better (and Other People's Lives Better, Too)*, John Murray, London, 2017
- Brad Stulberg and Steve Magness, *The Passion Paradox: A Guide to Going All In, Finding Success, and Discovering the Benefits of an Unbalanced Life*, Rodale Books, Pennsylvania, 2019
- Daniel Kahneman, *Thinking Fast and Slow*, Penguin, London, 2012
- Martin Seligman, *Authentic Happiness*, Penguin, Australia, 2011
- Martin Seligman, *Flourish*, Penguin, Australia, 2012
- David Allen, *Getting Things Done*, Penguin, Australia, 2014
- David J. Schwartz, *The Magic of Thinking Big*, Random House, London, 2016
- Eckhart Tolle, *A New Earth: Create a Better Life*, Penguin, London, 2016
- Joseph Murphy, *The Power of Your Subconscious Mind*, Prentice Hall Press, New Jersey, 2011

Articles and studies:

- 'Study: Are you too nice to be financially successful?', *The Ascent*, 4 October 2019
- Brian Tracy, 'Understanding Your Subconscious Mind', *Medium*, 10 November 2017
- Craig Lambert, 'The Science of Happiness', *Harvard Magazine,* January–February 2007
- Peter N. Stearns, 'The History of Happiness', *Harvard Business Review*, January–February 2012
- Shawn Achor, 'Positive Intelligence', *Harvard Business Review*, January–February 2012
- Andrew J. Oswald, 'Happiness and Productivity', *Journal of Labor Economics*, December 2009
- Brianna Wiest, '13 Ways to Start Training Your Subconscious Mind to Get What You Want', *Forbes*, 12 September 2018

TED Talks:

- Mihaly Csikszentmihalyi, 'Flow, the Secret To Happiness', TED2004 video on TED.com
- Dan Gilbert, 'The Surprising Science of Happiness', TED2004 video on TED.com
- Arianna Huffington, 'How to Succeed? Get More Sleep', TEDWomen 2010 video on TED.com
- David Steindl-Rast, 'Want to be Happy? Be Grateful', TEDEd 2013 video on TED.com
- Tim Urban, 'Inside the Mind of a Master Procrastinator', TED2016 video on TED.com
- Anil Seth, 'Your Brain Hallucinates Your Reality', TEDEd 2017 video on TED.com

Podcasts:

- Kara Loewentheil, *'Unf*ck Your Brain'*
- Amanda Seales, *'Small Doses'*
- Tim Ferriss, *'The Tim Ferriss Show'*
- Dax Shepard, *'Armchair Expert'*
- Sam Harris, *'Making Sense'*
- Scott Barry Kaufman, *'The Psychology Podcast'*
- Optimal Living Daily, *'Optimal Living Daily: Personal Development & Minimalism'*
- Oprah Winfrey, *'Oprah's SuperSoul Conversations'*
- Dacher Keltner, *'The Science of Happiness'*

Instagram:

- Dr Nicole LePera, *@the.holistic.psychologist*
- Sara Kubric, *@millennial.therapist*
- Nedra Glover Tawwab, *Therapist,* @nedratawwab
- Mia Mingus, *@mia.mingus*
- Bobo Matjila, *@bobo.matjila*
- Amanda E. White, *@therapyforwomen*
- Therapy for Black Girls ®, *@therapyforblackgirls*
- Brown Girl Therapy, *@browngirltherapy*
- *@subliming.jpg*

Personality tests:

- The Big Five, *Truity.com*
- The Four Temperaments (DISC), *Truity.com*
- Myers–Briggs Type Indicator (MBTI), *myersbriggs.org*
- Enneagram, Riso-Hudson Enneagram Type Indicator, *enneagraminstitute.com*

ABOUT THE AUTHOR

Ghanaian-Australian Lillian Ahenkan (aka FlexMami) is a multidisciplinary millennial making waves in the Australian entertainment industry. She's a DJ, MTV presenter, Build Series Sydney TV Presenter and has also lent her hosting skills to the likes of Vodafone, Pedestrian TV, VICE, MECCA, Samsung and Bumble.

In addition to this, she's a Social Commentator, Media Influencer, and Podcaster on Bobo and Flex, *Overshare* with Mamamia, *Whatever I Want* and the Spotify exclusive (and commissioned) Flex's *Semi Factual History Lessons. The Success Experiment* is Lillian's first book.

Passionate about bringing conversations surrounding taboo topics, pop culture, sexual liberation, critical thinking, identity, intersectionality and mental health to mainstream environments, Lillian is the CEO and Founder of conversation card game ReFlex (www.flexfactory.store), which does just that.

Her aim is to ensure everyone has the necessary tools and agency required to glow up and be their best self. Whatever that looks like for them and in whatever way that's possible in this economy.

She's been featured in *Vogue, i-D, Stylist, Elle, Grazia, Pedestrian TV, Daily Mail, Man Repeller* in addition to being a finalist for Cosmopolitan's Beauty Influencer of the Year 2018 and the winner of E Online's People's Choice Award for Influencer of The Year 2020.

LOST
THE
PLOT

A Lost the Plot book, first published in 2021 by Pantera Press Pty Limited
www.PanteraPress.com

Please send all permission queries to:
Pantera Press, P.O. Box 1989, Neutral Bay, NSW, Australia 2089 or info@PanteraPress.com

A Cataloguing-in-Publication entry for this book is available from the National Library of Australia.

ISBN 978-0-6489874-8-2 (Paperback)
ISBN 978-0-6489874-1-3 (eBook)

Cover and internal design: Elysia Clapin
Publisher: Lex Hirst
Editor: Anna Blackie
Proofreader: Cristina Briones
Author photo: Lillian Ahenkan
Printed and bound in China by Shenzhen Jinhao Colour Printing